Welcome to the United States

Bienvenue aux Etats-Unis

LAKES,

By Thomas O'Neill   Photographed by Michael S. Yamashita
Prepared by the Special Publications Division
National Geographic Society, Washington, D.C.

PEAKS, and PRAIRIES

Discovering the United States-Canadian Border

LAKES, PEAKS, AND PRAIRIES:
Discovering the United States-Canadian Border

By Thomas O'Neill
Photographed by Michael S. Yamashita

Published by The National Geographic Society
Gilbert M. Grosvenor, *President*
Melvin M. Payne, *Chairman of the Board*
Owen R. Anderson, *Executive Vice President*
Robert L. Breeden, *Vice President,
    Publications and Educational Media*

Prepared by The Special Publications Division
Donald J. Crump, *Editor*
Philip B. Silcott, *Associate Editor*
William L. Allen, *Senior Editor*
Mary Ann Harrell, *Consulting Editor*

Staff for this Book
Seymour L. Fishbein, *Managing Editor*
Charles E. Herron, *Picture Editor*
Marianne Rigler Koszorus, *Art Director*
Stephen J. Hubbard, *Senior Researcher*
Carolinda Hill, *Researcher*
Paul D. Kealey, *Research Assistant*
Jan Leslie Cook, Carolinda Hill, Jane R.
    McCauley, Tom Melham, Thomas O'Neill,
    Cynthia Russ Ramsay, Pamela Black Townsend,
    Picture Legend Writers
Elizabeth Ann Brazerol, Pamela Black Townsend,
    Editorial Assistants
Carol Rocheleau Curtis, *Illustrations Assistant*

Contents

JOHN D. GARST, JR., PATRICIA R. ISAACS, GARY M.
   JOHNSON, JOSEPH F. OCHLAK, *Map Research
   and Production*

Engraving, Printing, and Product Manufacture
ROBERT W. MESSER, *Manager*
GEORGE V. WHITE, *Production Manager*
MARY A. BENNETT, *Production Project Manager*
MARK R. DUNLEVY, DAVID V. SHOWERS, GREGORY STORER,
   GEORGE J. ZELLER, JR., *Assistant Production Managers*

JULIA F. WARNER, *Production Staff Assistant*

NANCY F. BERRY, DIANNE CRAVEN, LORI E. DAVIE,
   MARY ELIZABETH DAVIS, JANET A. DUSTIN,
   ROSAMUND GARNER, NANCY J. HARVEY, JOAN HURST,
   ARTEMIS S. LAMPATHAKIS, KATHERINE R. LEITCH,
   CLEO E. PETROFF, SHERYL A. PROHOVICH,
   NANCY E. SIMSON, VIRGINIA A. WILLIAMS,
   Staff Assistants

ANNE K. MCCAIN, *Index*

*Morris dancers banish winter spirits in Maine's Quoddy Head State Park, near the easternmost point of the United States.
Pages 2-3 and hardcover: The Maple Leaf and the Stars and Stripes—flags of friendship, flags of freedom.
Page 1: Pop art by Peter Max greets entrants at a border crossing.*

Foreword

Amid the euphoria that greeted the Canadian-assisted escape of United States hostages from Tehran in 1980 was a suggestion that Point Roberts—a detached piece of Washington State—be transferred to British Columbia. Even national gratitude did not extend that far. Countries, like private citizens, are jealous of their territory.

But boundaries between friendly people are not barriers; they invite contact and communication. Canadians are very conscious of this, for nearly all of them live less than a hundred miles or so from the border. In the Great Lakes region the boundary weaves a tangled course, dipping down to within 150 miles of the Mason-Dixon Line. No wonder a Fourth of July speaker in, say, Bismarck, North Dakota, expresses fraternal good wishes to his friends to the north, without realizing that a majority of Canadians are south of him.

In my work with the International Boundary Commission I have sensed the great geographical and social diversity of the border area between Canada and the lower forty-eight. It defines a legitimate scope of study. The section of boundary stretching from the southern tip of Alaska to the Arctic Ocean—vast and sparsely populated, evoking distant tales of Russian fur traders and the Klondike gold rush—is another world, another story. It is not included here.

Canada and the United States have more than a boundary in common; they share concerns over air pollution, the quality of fresh water, drug trafficking, and exploitation of seabed resources. Differences of national temperament and outlook do exist, though Canadians often appear ambivalent about them. Feelings about the United States range from awe, admiration, and envy to irritation, sometimes anger. There are fears of being swallowed up, of becoming a faint carbon copy of a dominant neighbor.

"Do you ever visit America?" friends in Europe ask me. I try to explain that Canada *is* American, that it's part of North America, that one should always speak of the United States, not America, when referring to that country. There are polite yawns of agreement, but nothing changes. Maybe Canadians are too self-conscious, too anxious to prove their distinct identity. And perhaps it was a little smug of me to tell a U.S. driver in the Canadian Yukon that the "lighters" she mispronounced at the gas pumps were part of the modern world's metric system, which her country was only slowly moving toward.

Shared concerns, differences in outlook and conditions of life, a rich tapestry of lakes, peaks, and prairies—this is the realm Tom O'Neill and Mike Yamashita explore in the pages that follow.

ALEC C. McEwen
Canadian Commissioner, International Boundary Commission

Boundary vista cleaves a Rocky Mountain forest where Montana (at left) meets Alberta in Waterton-Glacier International Peace Park.

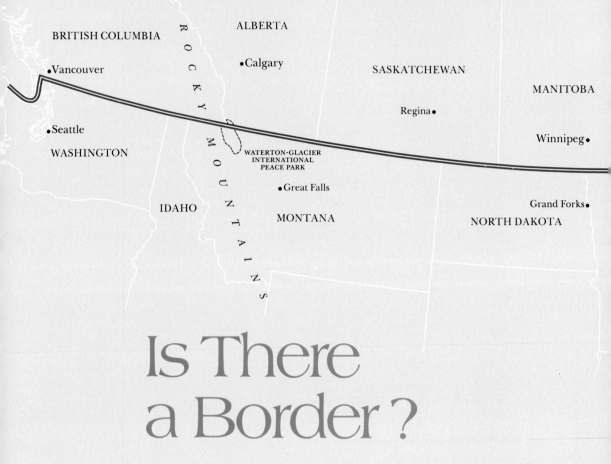

Is There
a Border ?

An Introduction

What border? For Montana farmer Dennis Iverson, no border existed
the day he got a call that a fire was spreading in Alberta only a few
miles north of his home. As a fire marshal for Liberty County, Iverson hurried to the World War II Army fire truck in his yard and rolled into Canada, not even stopping at the border station. Explanations could wait.

Where's a border? Handliners in Passamaquoddy Bay between Maine and
New Brunswick ask themselves this question whenever the pollack start running. Canadian waters and United States waters are one and the same as fishermen from both countries crisscross the border in boats in pursuit of the
migrating fish. Even when a patrol boat answers the question, the reply does not
sink in. A few days later the border jumpers resume their old pursuits.

Whose border? Ojibwa Indians believe they are merely passing through their
own territory when they leave the Windigo Islands in Ontario and cross Lake of
the Woods to pick up mail or shop in Angle Inlet, Minnesota. The Indians rarely entertain the thought that they have gone from one country to another.

The point of view is much the same in towns along the border. Crossing

Through forest, swamp, and plain, over mountain peaks and more than 2,000 miles of water runs the 3,987-mile boundary, its course set down in a series of 205 official maps. Out of more than a century of harsh contention, including two wars, grew an enduring peace, a unique bond that underpins the tradition of the longest undefended border in the world.

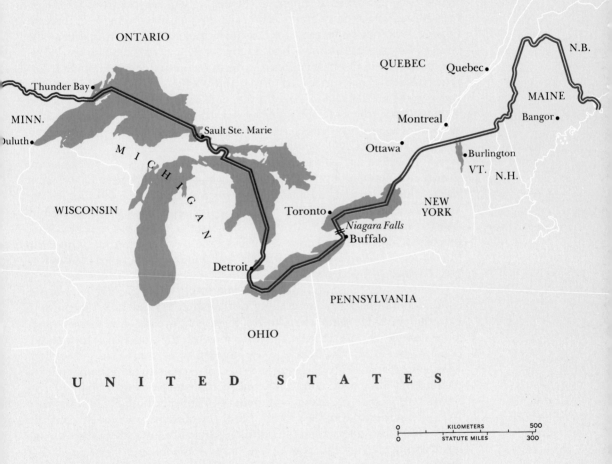

back and forth, observed a resident of Derby Line, Vermont, is "as natural as breathing air." But I know better. As I drove, flew, paddled, and hiked the U.S.-Canadian line from Maine and New Brunswick to Washington and British Columbia, I came to learn that the border is an inescapable presence. Some 120 customs stations alone guarantee its visibility. To be sure, citizens of Canada and the United States do not need a passport to travel between the two countries, and at the rural crossings it is not uncommon for a customs official simply to wave local folk through. Yet the border does make itself known. There is still duty to be paid for what to many people amounts to a local shopping trip. And I, for one, always felt the weight of the border whenever my car was searched, or when data was fed into a computer to check whether I had a criminal record.

Stretching from the Atlantic to the Pacific for a total of 3,987 miles, the border has acquired too many roles and symbols to be ignored or taken for granted. Where it divides four of the Great Lakes, the border area doubles as a central shipping channel between the Atlantic and the heartland of the continent. In the east the border acts as an audacious intruder, cutting through living rooms, backyards, even a cemetery. The border stands as a barrier for the increasing number of immigrants who try to slip illegally into the U.S. through Canada. It becomes a turnstile for consumers looking for the cheapest gas, the freshest fish, the latest-closing bars, or the fastest mail service. The border reminds some of an absentee landlord, as decisions on trade agreements and currency valuations, made in far-off Ottawa and Washington, D.C., influence daily traffic in the border region. And for the more than 25 million people who live within an hour's drive of the line, the border may serve as a vital reminder of the peaceful relations between the second largest (Canada) and the fourth largest (the U.S.) countries in the world.

At one time the international boundary did seem invisible. So vague was the demarcation that fortifications being built by Americans near Lake Champlain suddenly were abandoned in 1818, when a survey indicated that the site was in Canada. In the late 1800s on the northern grasslands, a church built by hand by Ukrainian immigrants invited to Manitoba turned out to rest on Minnesota soil. Such miscalculations are all but impossible now. Markers punctuate the border at least every mile and a half, and where the boundary crosses forests, a distinct 20-foot-wide strip, called a vista, is cleared.

From spring to winter I hugged the line, trying to keep within ten miles on either side. In the case of some larger cities such as Toronto and Vancouver, I extended my range slightly so as to visit them. By traveling close to the boundary, I was able to observe the many ways in which the presence of an international border affects the lives of those who live in its unusual neighborhood. What I also saw was a geographical and cultural microcosm of the two countries, conveniently displayed along a narrow, continent-spanning corridor. I witnessed a procession of small towns, most of them with tranquil settings, finely combed histories, and restless youth. The throb of industry sounded along the Great Lakes with smokestack cities on shore and enormous cargo ships on water. Dynamic metropolises rose up out of the countryside . . . Toronto, one of the most livable cities in North America . . . Detroit, a game, blue-collar bastion fighting to retain its industrial prominence. Woodlands and fields gave way to wilderness—unspoiled lakes by the thousand, a tumult of mountains. On the mist-hung Pacific shore, the seductive laid-back western style unfolded in Vancouver. And along the entire length of the border there were people of nearly every ethnic strain in the world.

Before I began my trip, I wondered if the two sides of the border would look and feel different. Like most Americans, I was conditioned to believe that Canada was essentially a twin of the U.S., except that Canada's winters were colder and its citizens preferred hockey to baseball. Stereotypes and blind spots disappear quickly on a border journey, though. Differences between the two countries are sometimes obvious; north of the line speed limits and distances are listed in kilometers—but spelled kilometres—and the highway signs appear in English and French: "Welcome to Canada/*Bienvenue au Canada*." The nation uses the metric system and both English and French are official languages. A few differences are dramatic, as in certain eastern areas when one passes from reserved New England into buoyant French Canada.

Other distinctions operate on a more subtle level. Canadian novelist Robertson Davies senses the impact of the northern environment: "What makes us different is climate," he told me. "We don't relate to the south like Americans, but to the north; and thus we are much more aware of climate. Canada is one of the few countries where the climate is positively dangerous; one can freeze to death not far out of Toronto. All this ends up making us more morose, more inward-turning, more melancholy. It makes us more like Scandinavians in nature than like the British or the Americans."

History also separates the two countries. One gained its nationhood by revolution, the other by evolution. Even today Elizabeth II, as Queen of Canada, is the symbolic ruler. One of the most fondly repeated descriptions of the U.S.-Canadian boundary hails it as the longest undefended border in the world. It is also a fact, however, that until they became allies during World War I, Canada and the United States were often contentious rivals. Through most of the 1800s, U.S. politicians talked longingly of annexing all or part of Canada. Even in the 1920s, each nation still had on the books counterattack plans in case of an invasion by the other. With Canada's population one-tenth that of the U.S., many Canadians still believe they are in danger of being overwhelmed by their neighbor; but now the weapons are economic and cultural.

During this century the U.S. and Canada have moved forward to establish firm and friendly relations. Their two-way trade is the largest in the world, exceeding a hundred billion dollars a year. The two countries have cooperated on massive public works projects, such as the construction of the St. Lawrence Seaway and the development of hydroelectric power at Niagara Falls. Defense pacts tie the nations together as well. The friendship is still prey to serious quarrels, however, as seen in Canada's anger over what it regards as a paltry U.S. effort against acid rain. But the crucial international bond will hold. As Arthur Meighen, a former prime minister, said, "We are not in the same boat, but we are pretty much in the same waters."

All told, some 142 years and 17 treaties and other agreements went into creating the border between southern Canada and the U.S. Some of the reasons for its precise position are no longer pressing. Still, it remains a respected entity, serving, in the words of Winston Churchill, as "an example to every country and a pattern for the future of the world."

I confess that my favorite times on the border often came when I could forget the border, the time, for example, when I canoed through deep woods on the St. Croix River between Maine and New Brunswick. No official was going to step from behind a tree and check my ID. But I also relished the summer day when I stood in a border wheat field, surrounded by miles of identical wheat fields. Looking around to gain my bearings, I spied in the distance a grain elevator painted a loud orange color, as the elevators in Canada typically are. Instantly I knew which side of the border I stood on. *Vive la différence.*

LIVING ON THE LINE   *St. Andrews, a New Brunswick resort town, shares Passamaquoddy Bay with neighbors*

in Maine; fish in these waters ignore the border—and so, at times, do fishermen.   13

Grain carrier calls at Thunder Bay, Ontario, for a cargo of prairie gold. Through

locks and canals the St. Lawrence Seaway-Great Lakes system links the heartland to the ocean. 15

BY PADDLE AND PORTAGE *Silvery arc dips to a border lake, where anglers can cast for bass, walleye, and pike*

in two countries—with fishing permits from Ontario and Minnesota.

A CHANCE FOR PARADISE   *Late-season soil treatment works an early snowfall into a North Dakota field.*

Freedom and farmland lured thousands of immigrants to the northern grasslands.   19

TO TOUCH THE SKY   *Climbers scale the rubbly scree of Mount Cleveland on the Montana side of Waterton-*

Glacier International Peace Park. The border lies six miles north of Cleveland's summit.

THE OTHER SIDE OF THE MOUNTAINS   *Carmanah Point Light beams from Vancouver Island, bracketing*

the rough passage into the Strait of Juan de Fuca with Cape Flattery Light in Washington.   23

Living
on the Line

From Passamaquoddy to the St. Lawrence

The word spread quickly through the two villages on Canada's Campobello Island: Customs was cracking down—this time on the grocery duty. Threatening news. For nearly all of the island's 1,400 residents, crossing the half-mile international bridge into Lubec, Maine, without worrying about strict car searches seemed nothing less than a basic right.

Sure, the islanders admitted, shoppers stretched the limits now and then and sneaked back groceries without paying the required Canadian duty. Why not? The Maine side had all the local stores. To buy Canadian, the islanders would have to drive 55 miles and back—with four border crossings thrown in.

The Canadians chose carefully their mode of protest. More than a hundred vehicles mobilized at a Lubec market on a warm July day when the governor of Maine was to attend a meeting on the island. Each shopper bought groceries worth slightly more than $15—the daily amount allowed before Canada would levy the import tax. When all had finished their meticulous buying, they returned en masse to the bridge, confessing that they owed money and politely demanding an itemized check of every grocery bag. The paperwork broke the back of the system. Bridge traffic stalled for nearly eight hours. The governor, caught in the jam, had to walk across. Next day the islanders awoke to the old ways on the bridge. Of course, the policy wouldn't last forever; in time officials would again intensify the search for taxable groceries. In the spring of 1984 the levy came to some 13 percent.

I heard the story of the protest from a few years back on my first day on Campobello, and I thought with pleasure that the Canadians had thrown their very own Boston Tea Party, protesting with conviction and theatricality against the revenue collectors. But while admiring the rebellious flair of the islanders, I also sympathized with the customs officials. They were trained to enforce the letter of the law, but in remote places like Campobello they found themselves struggling to observe the spirit of it as well.

What the manual neglected to teach, I gathered from the Campobello tale, was that the people who live along the line like to believe in the myth of the invisible border. True, there was a necessary pause at the crossing, but the locals tended to dismiss it as if it were just another (Continued on page 30)

The way west beckons brightly on Passamaquoddy Bay, where the boundary turns inland to weave a sunset course across the breadth of the continent.

*Q*uest for cod, which lured Old World fishing fleets in the 16th century, still busies watermen of Passamaquoddy. Ross Malloch out of Campobello Island, New Brunswick, gaffs a 30-pounder hooked on a longline. From a trawler—like those tied up at the island (opposite)—the crew retrieves a line two miles long with 2,500 squid-baited hooks. "The Coast aboundeth with such multitudes of Codd that the inhabitants of New England doe dung their ground with Codd," wrote a 17th-century colonist, "and it is a commodity better than the golden mines of the Spanish Indies." Such bounty spurred historic conflicts between European powers. Even today Canada and the United States argue over fishing rights on Georges Bank east of Cape Cod.

PRECEDING PAGES: *Maine lobsterman pulls a dinghy to his Jonesport boat, a spare, clean-hulled design familiar to Passamaquoddy folk since the 1920s. Open side of the wheelhouse lets the boatman reach out to haul up lobster pots.*

traffic light. "We didn't ask that border to be placed here," grumbled a man in Lubec. "We have to function as one community."

I had entered the diverse and sensitive world of the border, populated by unintentional diplomats and grounded in the intrigues of history and politics. Here in its eastern sector it threads the dark evergreen woodlands—no longer the "forest primeval" of Longfellow's Acadia, but instead a vast spread of commercial timberland. It is a world of tough woodcutters, of mill towns and fishing towns and narrow-shouldered farmsteads, their rectangular shapes fixed by riparian needs. Here I would meet people living on the line, their homes straddling it. I would visit communities flavored by French culture, and patrol with lawmen who track illegal immigrants. A myth? A bother? I found the border a fascinating reality.

It begins out in the choppy North Atlantic in the rich fishing grounds of Georges Bank, where the 200-mile offshore limits of both countries intersect. The line enters the continent at Passamaquoddy Bay, where remarkable 28-foot tides surge in and out. Here it passes West Quoddy Head, easternmost point of the contiguous United States, and the candy-striped lighthouse that rises on a bluff like a giant barbershop pole.

Along a narrow tidal channel sits Lubec, looking like many New England coastal towns: clam diggers bent over moist flats, a rickety wooden pier for fishing boats, verandaed white frame houses. At one time there were more than 20 sardine factories in the vicinity; only two remain. The town wears its decline openly, with a main street of boarded-up shops. "Sardines used to be the lunchbox food for coal miners, crop pickers, and factory workers," mused Robert Peacock, third-generation president of R. J. Peacock Canning Co. "People don't work that way any more, though. There's all this prepared food, and factories now have cafeterias. Even yet, when a car factory shuts down, we feel it."

Across the narrows the people of Campobello continue to survive primarily on fishing. At the piers hammering sounded from the holds as fishermen readied their boats for the springtime herring run off Nova Scotia.

Roosevelt Campobello International Park enshrines the summer home of Franklin D. Roosevelt; he was stricken with polio on the island in 1921. Near the international bridge, Snug Cove marks the site where Benedict Arnold stayed for a time after the Revolutionary War. A brave, battle-tested general for the 13 Colonies, Arnold married a British sympathizer in 1779 and promptly exchanged his loyalties, informing the British of an American plan to invade Canada. Ever since, he has been regarded as the epitome of treason in the United States, but in Canada I heard him described as a hero.

The border disappears in the minds of many local fishermen, particularly those who handline for pollack and cod and sell them to markets and restaurants. In Eastport, Maine, I talked with handliner Reid Wilson as he stood in his living room with high rubber boots on, peering through binoculars at the waters of Passamaquoddy Bay.

"I don't see many sea gulls sitting on the water yet," he said, "but when they get thick that means the flood tide is bringing in a lot of little organisms to feed on. Then I know that the pollack won't be far behind."

Canadians and Americans are supposed to fish in their own waters. But,

*Traditions of New France, New England, old England, and Indian cultures mingle
at the winding borderline. For more than half a century 7.7 million acres lay in dispute
(between the U.S. claim in blue and the British in red); in 1842 Daniel Webster and
Lord Ashburton set the boundary in the treaty that bears their names.*

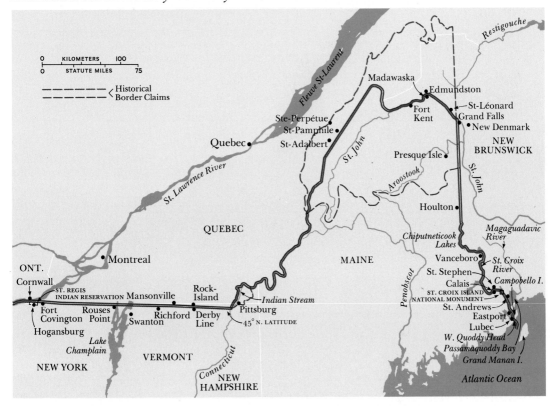

said Reid, if he has to hook pollack on the Canadian side, he will. How often had
the Canadians chased him back across the line? Reid smiled: "Not once during
the last two years. It all depends on how relations are." He thought a recent
meeting between leaders of the two nations would make for a good year.

Who may fish where has ruffled tempers along this coast for centuries. It
was a major stumbling block in peace talks after the American Revolution. In recent years a dispute arose over fishing rights on Georges Bank, where territorial
claims overlap and oil and natural gas resources are also an issue. In 1984 the
International Court of Justice set the boundary in the disputed area.

From Passamaquoddy Bay the boundary angles inland, veering and jag-
ging up the St. Croix River for some 129 miles. I hugged the riverbank on a
Maine road and soon came to Calais, which faces its twin, St. Stephen, across the
river. Two towns in two different countries, they have embraced in an unusually
tight way. In Calais I noticed that almost every vehicle displayed New Brunswick
plates. The reason? Groceries were cheaper in Maine; so were lawn mowers and
microwave ovens, tennis rackets, and video games. This held true despite the
fact that the Canadian dollar was buying only 82 cents American. Canadian cars

lined up at the gas stations to save 50 cents a gallon. The year before gas in Canada was the bargain. New Brunswick plates showed up in front of the post office; the Canadians had discovered that mail traveled more cheaply in the States— even mail headed back to Canada.

Maine residents, meanwhile, were crossing the river to buy fresh fish, cheese, and wool clothes. Labels may vanish from the clothes as their new owners try to slip the goods back without paying duty. Having a baby was cheaper in Canada. Hospital rooms cost less, and the baby gains dual citizenship.

Water for Calais comes from St. Stephen, through a pipe under the bridge. The towns' fire departments answer each other's calls, and the hospitals send each other blood (duty free). The border did seem invisible here.

Such closeness made perfect sense to the young mayor of Calais, John Cashwell. I met him one day when he dropped from the sky in a helicopter he pilots for the Georgia-Pacific Corporation, the forest-products company that is the largest employer in the area. The mayor wore a tan jumpsuit and sported a droopy Lech Walesa-like mustache. "We and our neighbors are almost identical as far as distance from government and distance from supplies go," he explained. "It's that distance that created this interdependence."

Like many people in Calais, John was married to a Canadian. Such intermarriage has been going on since both banks of the river were settled in the late 1700s. Locals even have a word for someone who crosses the river to marry:

Day breaks over the easternmost promontory in the lower 48 states, where West Quoddy Head Light has warned mariners of perilous shallows since 1808. Whales and harbor seals glide through these waters, heedless of the boundary between this Maine shore and Campobello Island. Canada's farthest east lies some 800 miles beyond Quoddy.

overhomer. The original settlers hailed from southern Maine—then part of Massachusetts—and other corners of New England. Many on the British side called themselves Loyalists—diehard supporters of the crown who moved north after the Revolutionary War. Two centuries later, Anglophilia persists, with Union Jacks flying from private flagpoles and the strains of "God Save the Queen" closing civic meetings. Elizabeth II, by law, is Queen of Canada, though the nation governs itself. At the time of my visit people on both sides were eagerly awaiting the visit of Prince Charles and Princess Diana to the town of St. Andrews, where they would observe the 200th anniversary of the Loyalist arrival.

A stern test of cross-border friendship came with the War of 1812. Calais and St. Stephen promptly organized militias, but their citizens continued to row back and forth across the river. The St. Stephen militia even lent the U.S. side some gunpowder for a proper celebration of the Fourth of July.

Mayor Cashwell spoke of the hard times in his town as we flew over the Maine woods. Spotting a pair of bald eagle nests in the treetops, he joked ruefully: "Those are the only two housing starts we've had this year." He hoped to establish a regional promotion board with St. Stephen. But when politics and government spending enter the picture, the border evidently becomes quite visible. Complications multiply. In parting, the mayor asked me to guess how many agencies—from both nations—Calais had to contact in order to build a tidal diversion dam across the international river. The answer was 35.

Before the British settled this area, it was the French who envisioned the St. Croix Valley as a toehold for a North American empire. In 1604—three years before John Smith arrived at Jamestown—the Sieur de Monts, a Huguenot gentleman, led an expedition to begin colonizing the northern coast, which the French called Acadia. For the first site de Monts chose a small island in a river he named St. Croix—Holy Cross—for the way it branched out in the shape of a cross. After a bitter winter in which nearly half of his 79 men died of scurvy, de Monts moved the survivors to more hospitable terrain. The French soon directed their colonizing energies to the St. Lawrence Valley, where in 1608 de Monts's cartographer, Samuel de Champlain, founded the city of Quebec.

The Treaty of Paris in 1783 marked the St. Croix as a bound between the new United States and the British settlements. Trouble was, the negotiators were using old maps, and no river of that name was known any longer in the region. The British argued for the Schoodic, and the Americans for the Magaguadavic, ten miles to the east. The latter line would throw the Loyalists of St. Stephen and St. Andrews back into the United States. As a stalemate grew, Loyalists in 1797 unearthed piles of yellow bricks and foundation lines on an island in the Schoodic—apparent evidence of de Monts's settlement. Boundary arbitrators accepted the evidence and the name St. Croix returned to the maps. To still any lingering doubts, archaeologists returned in 1969. Sure enough, they found the bricks and foundations—even a fleur-de-lis pendant. Positioned on the Maine side of the river, the island has been named a U.S. national monument; both nations have taken steps to declare it an international historic site.

Before I left the St. Croix I joined a canoeing party on the upper reaches. Four of us, including a guide, shoved off on a soggy spring morning from Vanceboro, Maine, where the St. Croix issues from the Chiputneticook Lakes. The river courses through a monochromatic landscape of pines, firs, and spruces broken occasionally by a stark white stand of birch or an uninviting bog.

A Georgia-Pacific timber tract brackets the river and company dams affect the river's flow. For the many lovers of the outdoors in the area, the St. Croix represents a success story. Effluent from a pulp and paper mill downstream at Woodland had steadily fouled the river. A century of logging use had deposited other pollutants and had degraded the habitat. Fish were disappearing and an acrid stench arose from the dark-foamed water. Hunting and fishing camps closed down. In the late 1960s, as environmentalist efforts intensified,

England's—and Canada's—future queen greets well-wishers in St. Andrews, haven for Loyalists who left the newly independent United States. Princess Diana and Prince Charles visited the New Brunswick town during its bicentènnial celebration in 1983.

FOLLOWING PAGES: New England charmer, built more than a century ago, perches above the St. Croix River amid a profusion of dandelions. On a nearby island the Sieur de Monts in 1604 founded a settlement whose ruins helped fix the boundary line.

antipollution steps began to revive the river. Canoeists and sportsmen gradually returned. Migratory Atlantic salmon—once the staple of the Passamaquoddy Indians and the colonists—were reintroduced. Georgia-Pacific has added fish ladders to its dams so the salmon can return upstream.

I found the upper St. Croix an intimate river, with just enough rips, boulders, and hairy stories about dumpings to make it invigorating. Our Maine guide was Martin Brown, and he looked the part with his patched wool pants, plaid lumberjack coat, slouch hat, broad shoulders, and thick mustache.

Martin was a devotee of the old technique of poling. Standing in the middle of *Annabelle* with his legs shoulder-width apart, he wielded an ash pole more than twice his height. He pushed against the riverbed with the rhythmic stroke of a cross-country skier, propelling his canoe through the rapids. Thus he paid homage to the men who used to work the log drives on the St. Croix, deftly wielding poles to maneuver bateaux and untangle logjams.

This was the true way, Martin insisted. "When they hear of poling," he said, "people think of the Cajuns down in the bayou or the old guys up north. But poling's the only way to be truly sensitive to the current." Gaining my feet in the canoe one day, I tried the technique and was surprised at the maneuverability the long pole provided. Depending on the way I pushed it off the bottom or planted it for leverage, I could slide off a small wave and turn the canoe. "After you've poled, it will be pedestrian to sit down and paddle again," Martin called out. I wasn't prepared to believe yet. Hearing the rumble of a rapid ahead, I dropped back to my knees and drove the paddle blade into the water.

From the St. Croix I moved north. Trees fell away and the countryside opened into rolling hills: potato country. It was the loamy soil, the agricultural agents explained, that accounted for this interruption of the woods. The spud belt straddled the border—forty miles wide by a hundred miles long.

When settlers cleared the forests here in the mid-1800s, they discovered they could grow corn, beans, potatoes, and clover. Potatoes quickly became king, though. Farmers in this part of Maine's Aroostook County saw that their potatoes could satisfy the growing starch industry, which was booming hand in hand with the manufacture of cotton. Maine potatoes soon accounted for 90 percent of the nation's starch. A one-crop economy took root. Today the region specializes in seed and table potatoes. Each year, however, demand grows for processed spuds, such as French fries and potato chips, to which Maine's round white varieties are not as well suited as those of the western United States. Once the leading producer of potatoes, Maine now tallies only about 8 percent of the nation's crop. And cheaper imports from New Brunswick are slicing into Maine's already shrunken market. Protesting Maine farmers in 1980 went so far as to block eight border crossings, dumping tons of potatoes.

Driving through the Aroostook in mid-May, I observed a tranquil scene, tractors inching along the horizon as farmers planted the fields. In the fall the schools would let out, as they always have in potato country, so that the children could join the harvest, handpicking Kennebecs, Katahdins, Superiors, Atlantics, Ontarios, Sebagos, and Russet Burbanks.

Farmers grumbled to me about low prices, bad weather, expensive machinery, and uninterested children. It struck me that thus far on the border the local

Neighborly ties, nurtured since the late 1700s, join Calais, Maine (foreground), and St. Stephen, New Brunswick, across the St. Croix. They share fire fighters, water supplies, and Independence Day festivities. In the War of 1812 they shared a Methodist preacher who persuaded both towns to declare a separate peace.

economies had nearly all been dependent on natural resources—fish, timber, and soil. And two centuries of such dependence have taken a toll. Many of the towns, particularly in Maine, wore a frayed look, with the weather-beaten, once-grand frame houses reminding me somehow of slumped shoulders. And so it was that mayors and city managers along the way talked bravely of their hopes for tourism, counting on one always vital resource—beautiful scenery.

At Grand Falls, New Brunswick, the St. John River replaced potato fields as the border indicator. Just as definitively, English gave way to French. The transition startled me with its abruptness. Suddenly the bakery became *la pâtisserie,* and the drugstore, *la pharmacie. Buvez Coca-Cola*—Drink Coca-Cola—an advertisement urged me. Cafe patrons chatted in French while watching the morning news in English. The city even had a boulevard for its main street.

Up the road in St-Léonard—rhymes with leotard—a lofty cathedral-style Catholic church ruled the town center. Main Street was now Rue Principale and signs to the border read *La Frontière.* The border corridor on the Canadian side had become an extensive French neighborhood, and so it would continue for the next 600 miles to the St. Lawrence River (Fleuve St-Laurent, to French speakers). Despite the great tide of English settlement and administration in Canada, the French Canadians had preserved their cultural legacy. And they cling to it proudly in much of the area that French kings once claimed as New France (Quebec) and Acadia (Nova Scotia and New Brunswick).

In the United States, with its melting pot ethos, French culture has not survived as strongly as it has in Canada. Yet I often heard the liquid sounds of French on streets and in homes in northern Maine. The people on both sides of the St. John still feel a common bond, distinguishing their region with the name Madawaska, after a tributary of the St. John.

About a fourth of Canada's people claim French as their mother tongue. And in 1969 the country decided to have two official languages. The manifestations range from traffic signs in both languages to a bilingual federal civil service and official encouragement of French language and culture.

One day in Edmundston, a New Brunswick town of 12,000 on the St. John, customs broker Fernand Nadeau told me of the ways in which the French-speaking community flavors local life. "You go around at two or three in the morning, and there will be people in the restaurants," he said. "Across the border and to the south they roll up the sidewalks at nine o'clock. We're night birds here." Nadeau also informed me that Madawaskan women were widely known for their stylish appearance. For a small town the young women did present a chic air with their wide-shouldered blouses and their tight, cropped pants—which were à la mode in Paris as well. I enjoyed bilingual Edmundston. After the stolid towns I had encountered up to now, the people here seemed exceptionally outgoing and talkative.

Though the French-Canadian culture remains strong and vibrant, Jean-Louis Boucher, editor of the weekly *Le Madawaska*, expressed concern about living so close to the United States with its powerful siren songs in English. "You take television at my house," he said in French-accented English. "I have four girls and I am lucky to have two TVs. I couldn't listen to the French news otherwise. English has such a big influence that it's easy to get assimilated." The editor sighed and leaned back in his leather chair. "It all depends on our bilingual school system. If the children don't continue speaking French, it will disappear and we will eliminate ourselves."

Boucher could have been speaking directly to the other side of the St. John. In the mill town of Madawaska, Maine, the school system is actively trying to salvage French. Less than 20 years ago pupils were punished for speaking French on school grounds—even though a majority of the youngsters came from Francophone families. Then, in the early 1970s, the schools established some of the first bilingual programs in the nation. Today in the town of Madawaska all students in the system, some 1,100, are enrolled in bilingual study.

I also enrolled for a session one day, squeezing behind a pint-size desk at the Evangeline School (named for the Acadian heroine of Longfellow's poem). "Melissa, *montrez-moi le drapeau*," began instructor Beverly Madore. "*C'est le drapeau!*" cried a dark-haired first grader, pointing to the flag. "Shawn," Mrs. Madore called, "*Ferme la porte.*" Shawn hesitated, then flew to the front of the room and closed the door.

"Once we go over the material," Mrs. Madore told me later, "I'll switch on and off in English and French so the words don't seem so foreign. That's how we speak in the valley, a few words in English and then a few words in French."

During my visit to the St. John border towns in New Brunswick and Maine I thought with pleasure that for once the David Canada was influencing the Goliath United States; the vital French culture and bilingual programs on the northern side of the river provided a model for communities to the south. And that is one export that will never show up in the commerce tables.

The St. John River was probably not even the border that negotiators had in mind when they drew up the lines. In the Treaty of Paris they ran the boundary north from the source of the St. Croix River to the highlands that mark the divide of the St. Lawrence drainage. But where were those highlands?

The Colonies' peace commissioners—an illustrious group that included Benjamin Franklin, John Adams, and John Jay—negotiated with maps that were imprecise in some places and totally wrong in others. Boundary instructions ended up as inevitably vague. The diplomats of the Revolution saw their duty as establishing the broad outlines of a new nation; the fine details could be worked out later. As settlers drifted into the northern wilds in the 19th century, the British and Americans found themselves at loggerheads. Yes, where were those highlands? The United States placed them up near the St. Lawrence, on the watershed between it and the Restigouche River—a boundary that would parallel the St. Lawrence, reaching as close as 33 miles to the city of Quebec.

The British diplomats were appalled; the American line would deprive them of the strategic St. John River link between the cities of Quebec and Halifax, as well as valuable timberland that supplied the "King's Masts" to the Royal Navy. The British put the highlands to the south, on a line that would have lopped off a third of the Maine we know today. People in the disputed territory began to claim squatter's rights. Between 1839 and 1841 the region bristled with militias and forts as Maine and New Brunswick each sought to intimidate the other. This bloodless standoff became known as the Aroostook War. A blockhouse built by a Maine posse still stands in Fort Kent, on the St. John.

I look with some nostalgia at a time when two powers could allow more than 50 years to pass without fixing a boundary—and without a single loss of life in the area. Not until 1842 did Secretary of State Daniel Webster, under President John Tyler, and Webster's counterpart, Lord Ashburton, compromise on the St. John as the border, giving Maine its familiar peaked-hat shape.

A deciding factor in the Webster-Ashburton Treaty negotiations was a curious map discovered by the American historian Jared Sparks. It showed a bold red line, purportedly drawn by Ben Franklin, which gave the area in question to the British. The impatient Webster used the map to force the new and headstrong state of Maine to compromise. Allegations have arisen—and they have been stoutly denounced—that British money, passed to Webster, smoothed the way to compromise. For students of border history the controversy was revived as recently as 1933, with the discovery of yet another old map. This one, said to have been inscribed by John Jay, supported the original American claim.

After the St. John River the border turns south and disappears once again into the woods, along the highlands the two powers finally agreed on. To reach the border I had to drive to the St. Lawrence and then double back on narrow roads through the Quebec countryside. Hardly anyone spoke English now. In Quebec, French is the only official language, by virtue of a provincial law enacted in 1977. It came amid a surging French-Canadian nationalism that also produced an abrasive campaign for an independent Quebec. The language law, though born of historic grievances against Anglophone dominance, caused confusion and anxiety within the English-speaking population—11 percent of the province, according to 1981 census figures. Court challenges and new provincial legislation have relaxed some provisions of the original law.

I drove through towns only two or three streets wide. Most places were named after saints I had never heard of—St-Omer, Ste-Perpétue, St-Adalbert. This was "longlot" farm country. The pattern of long, narrow fields dates back to the 17th century, when elongated plots were laid out to give each farm access to the waterways. In the fields rocks uncovered by plowing were piled up like ancient Celtic burial mounds. Farmhouses, many painted in purples, blues, and greens, shouldered up next to one another; there was none of the spaciousness associated with farmland in the States. Every few miles a religious shrine or a cross appeared alongside the road. All this changed at the border. On the U.S. side stretched dark spruce forests, the domain of lumber and paper companies. There were no towns, no paved roads, no tilled soil. The few French-Canadian towns at the border revolved around noisy mills with their acres of stacked logs. The lumber to feed the mills was cut by Canadians in Maine, then shipped from the mills to the Middle East.

In the end-of-the-road town of St-Pamphile, farmhouses and barns stood right on the main road, scenting the air with hay and manure. On the town fringe, by contrast, large lumber trucks rumbled into a computerized mill, where a laser directed the saw cuts. Just one step over the line from St-Pamphile I discovered an enclave of Americans. Their cluster of houses immediately behind the border station reminded me of wagons drawn together on the prairie. The population of 25 included a game warden, a customs official, a fire warden, an owner of a small lumber company, and their families. Located 55 miles from the nearest hardtop road in the States, this tiny community used Canadian schools and stores; most of its inhabitants spoke better French than English. But there was no confusion of identity. They celebrate the Fourth of July each year. "We live in the United States," declared forester Bruce Marquis, "and we will always think of ourselves as American citizens."

Farther south, on the New Hampshire-Quebec border, where the Connecticut River headwaters rise, a group of settlers some 150 years ago were so confused about which country they belonged to that they went ahead and established their own nation. The Indian Stream Republic, named for a local watercourse, spanned 250 square miles, had its own constitution, legislature, and a 40-man militia. It lasted nearly four years, from 1832 to 1835, before the New Hampshire militia invaded and imposed state laws. The Webster-Ashburton Treaty finally settled matters, ceding the land to the United States.

The border today is clearly laid out. On land a marker appears every mile or so. The markers range from three-inch bronze tablets to a 19-foot-high portal on the Pacific shore. The most common are obelisks of concrete, granite, or stainless steel, standing four or five feet high. At times the border becomes a sharply visible fact—a 20-foot-wide cleared   (Continued on page 50)

Twin feed silos pierce the haze in the dairy and grain country of the St. John River Valley. Here the border leaves river courses and runs north, a 78-mile stretch flanked by the Trans-Canada Highway and the last—or first—stretch of old U.S. 1.

*P*atchwork of terraced fields patterns the New Brunswick countryside, part of the potato domain that spreads into Maine's giant Aroostook County. Boundary feuding here in the late 1830s produced the Aroostook War—a war mainly of words, ended by diplomacy. The resulting line turns westward near Grand Falls, New Brunswick (below), into the French-speaking Madawaska country. There proud villages trace their history to "le grand dérangement" — England's eviction of the Acadians from Nova Scotia in 1755. Historian Alexander Savoie (left) of Edmundston has recorded their struggle to preserve French identity; today the "République du Madawaska" unites citizens on both sides of the boundary.

FOLLOWING PAGES: Waking gently, the St. John flows toward Grand Falls (background), with its 140-foot cataract. On just such a morning, perhaps, the legendary Maliseet Indian, Malabeam, guided her Mohawk captors to their doom here. As their canoes drifted, they slept. The roar of Grand Falls roused them, the tale goes, but too late. Over they went, 200 raiders, along with courageous Malabeam.

CHARLES E. HERRON, NATIONAL GEOGRAPHIC STAFF

*C*lipping the hedge: Odette Lepage-Barnes heads an International Boundary
Commission crew hacking overgrowth from the 20-foot boundary swath along
the 45th parallel. Permanently established in 1925, the IBC assumes the unending task
of grooming the world's longest unfortified border. One obstacle encountered: Rocks piled
by farmers clearing land a century ago. Early surveyors painstakingly measured with
chronometers carried by sled or canoe; a modern-day team computes distances with a
theodolite and electronic equipment (opposite, above). Among its other tasks the IBC
maintains some 8,000 monuments; one near Houlton, Maine (opposite), gets a face-lift.

swath, or vista, slicing into forests. Where the boundary follows a water channel, reference monuments on shore are used to calculate the position of the line. The precision of measurement reaches down to a hundredth of a second of longitude—about eight inches of land or water in these latitudes.

The task of keeping the boundary a clean and well-marked place falls to the International Boundary Commission (IBC), permanently established in 1925 in the last important treaty dealing with the subject. Each country appoints a commissioner whose staff carries out the seemingly ceaseless job of clearing vistas and repairing monuments. At one time the grooming techniques included spraying the vistas with herbicides. Concern over the unknown effects of these chemicals—among them was an ingredient of the controversial Agent Orange—halted the practice in 1978.

"Welcome to the 45th parallel!" Field engineer Odette Lepage-Barnes, a member of Canada's IBC staff, greeted me on a dirt road near Richford, Vermont. After a firm handshake Odette led me up a muddy slope to see her Québecois lumberjacks cutting through a dense growth of poplar and maple saplings with their chain saws. "We have 68 kilometers (42 miles) to clear this season," she reported. "And when it's 68 kilometers of up and down, it's no gift."

"Look!" Odette instructed at the top of a hill. I looked down a recently cleared vista that headed due west; then I followed her finger to see the line suddenly veering up a mountain to the north. The 45th parallel seemed to wander all over the countryside. Odette laughed at my confusion.

"It is said that the early surveyors were drunk," smiled IBC Commissioner Alec McEwen in his Ottawa office when I queried him about the crooked parallel. "I know that there were references made to barrels of rum on the requisition list. But, really, I think they did a respectable job." The 45th parallel, dividing the two nations for 155 miles, is the oldest part of the boundary, having been surveyed before the Revolutionary War to separate New York State from Lower Canada—today's province of Quebec. The surveyors relied on magnetic compasses as they toiled through the wilderness, notching trees as border marks.

"The line is not only crooked, but it goes too far north," confessed McEwen. In fact the line strays as much as one and a quarter miles into Canada. "Angry members of Parliament seeing it on a topographical map will write in and ask why we don't move the border," he said with amusement. "I tell them that it's a fundamental principle that the original markers determined the line, mainly for purposes of stability. You can't move it for every mathematical correction."

"Besides," McEwen added, "if the 45th is too far north, the 49th parallel in the west is too far south in places. We've computed the discrepancies, and Canada comes out ahead on the western boundary."

The most peculiar feature of the 45th is the way it trespasses through lives and properties. In the Siamese-twin towns of Derby Line, Vermont, and Rock-Island, Quebec, the parallel runs smack through the community, affecting life like a house guest who refuses to leave. There is no such thing as an aimless stroll through the border neighborhood. It is easy to mistakenly cross the border when crossing a street. The only times residents can cross without reporting to customs officials are when they attend church on Sunday, have tickets to summer theater at the opera house, or go to the library. The 450-seat opera hall and library are housed in a handsome building erected deliberately on the line in 1904, before anyone paid much attention to small-town border traffic. The stage is in Canada; most of the audience sits in the U.S. "The applause could be heard all the way to Canada," a favorable review might gush.

The building's international location has led to some famous incidents. When legal complications prevented the Beatles from appearing together in either country, a promoter tried unsuccessfully to reunite them in the opera house. The library once became the heavily guarded site of a hearing in a drug case. An official sat on a chair straddling the line and took oaths from a convicted informer on the Canadian side and from three accused smugglers caught in the States. None of them could have been legally held if they had managed to step into the other country.

One day, Mrs. Edward Gosselin, Sr., invited me into the ornate living room of her home, one of the so-called line houses. Mrs. Gosselin laughed as she demonstrated where the invisible border passed along the edge of the front room. "You see," she said, "I eat in Canada, sleep in Canada, and watch TV and go to the bathroom in the United States." Mrs. Gosselin told me she paid income tax to both countries, kept two mailing addresses, paid three-fourths of her property tax to Canada. Did the border bother her? "Not a bit," she replied.

During my journey along the 45th parallel I stopped in at a Border Patrol sector headquarters in Swanton, Vermont. The arrest of illegal immigrants had become a daily occurrence here, I was told by Larry Teverbaugh, the chief patrol agent. As the southern border of the U.S. turned into a wall to block a surge of illegal immigration, more and more of the would-be immigrants without visas resorted to the northern border. Fewer than a tenth of the 3,240 agents in the Border Patrol—the enforcement arm of the Immigration and Naturalization Service—were posted on the long Canadian border. Canada's immigration laws, less strict than those of the U.S., made it an attractive staging area for illegal entry to the south. Smugglers were charging $2,000 a head, said Teverbaugh. For special cases, Mafia members for example, "the price goes as high as $15,000," he added.

Teverbaugh showed me a room filled with the noise of teletypes and crackling radios. On the wall hung a Plexiglas "intrusion board" with schematic drawings of some 35 roads and paths that were outfitted with electronic and infrared sensors. Whenever a sensor was tripped, a light would flash for the appropriate area. The sector's most publicized catch came in 1978 when a young woman wanted for terrorist activities in Germany tried to walk into the United States. But with all the patrolling and electronic gadgetry, the Border Patrol estimates that it snares only a fraction of the illegal entrants on the northern border.

Despite the increased activity, life for Border Patrol agents here is normally as quiet as a month of Sundays. All of them have been tempered by at least two years of duty on the hectic Mexican border, where in 1983 some 1.1 million people were apprehended in contrast to about 9,000 on the Canadian border. Most agents, I was told, consider assignment to the northern border as a kind of professional R and R. "It takes a certain adjustment up here," admitted James Judd, recently back from a 45-day loan to a California border post north of Tijuana. "Some nights we would catch 2,000 aliens. Here I might catch one a day. You have to be very patient and be able to sit behind a building for perhaps your whole shift. Down there you don't sit still for ten minutes."

Different rooms mean different countries for Murray McFarlane. The line running through the obelisk divides his lawn and his home on the Richelieu River near Noyan, Quebec; he rests on the U.S. side. Flowing out of Lake Champlain, the Richelieu served as a highway for explorers and invading armies in centuries past. Along this section of the line on the 45th parallel, a hundred structures once straddled the line, many notorious as smugglers' dens. Line dwellers today find few discomforts in their unusual settings, despite such nuisances as dual income and property taxes and often two mailing addresses. At Mansonville, Quebec, the old customhouse (opposite), closed for lack of customers, went up for sale. Refurbished, it reopened as a vacation home.

Judd, a former Marine from Oklahoma, confessed that he and his friends sometimes missed the action and life-style on the southern border. Thus, when I accepted his invitation to dinner, it came as no surprise to sit down to a meal of tortillas, refried beans, jalapeño peppers, and chorizo, and listen to the company talking longingly of the Southwest. "We just get homesick once in a while," Judd remarked, reaching for the hot sauce.

The next morning I headed west, pausing at the intersection of the 45th parallel and the St. Lawrence. Here the broad, murky river cut in two a small Mohawk Indian reserve. On the U.S. side of the St. Regis reservation, in the town of Hogansburg, New York, a truck stop and bingo hall shared the main road with a traditional Iroquois longhouse.

As I looked about the reservation, I thought back to the Border Patrol, the twin towns and other places I had seen, and remembered all the attention, conscious and unconscious, that was paid to the border. I also realized that the habit of crossing it several times a day was wearing on me now and then. The officers never waved me through; often I was ordered into a small room where I explained what I planned to do and not do in Canada. It was like being stopped on the street every day and being asked for ID. In a sense, then, I envied the perspectives of some of the Mohawks at St. Regis. Jake Swamp, a traditional chief with a weary face and long black hair, told me he considered himself neither American nor Canadian. "We don't recognize the boundary," he said. "It's a

boundary line made between the United States and Great Britain. The governments want to portray us as citizens of either country, but we maintain that we're still an independent nation that has never given up its rights. We are members of the Hotinonshonni Nation—the Iroquois Confederacy."

Vaughn Aldrich, a Mohawk lawyer who represented the elected council on the Canadian side, stated emphatically, "We're North American Indians, that's what we are." Customs officials, he said, have at least made the gesture of creating a separate lane on the bridge over the St. Lawrence on heavy traffic days, so that Indians can pass back and forth with ease.

Crossing from Cornwall, Ontario, into the United States, I pondered briefly the notion of telling the customs man that my nationality was North American. But I faltered. What was a crucial distinction for the Indians' sense of identity was little more than an idealistic conceit for me. At the border I saw the badge, the gun, the fingers typing my license number into the computer, and I heard the voice: "What country are you a citizen of?"

"The United States," I admitted and, after a few more questions, drove away, vowing never to believe anyone who told me the border was invisible.

*I*nternational ambience: Summer patrons at the Dundee Line Hotel find the bar in Dundee, Quebec, the pool table in Fort Covington, New York, and the checkerboard in both. Enterprise began here in 1820, with a trading post catering to traffic on the Salmon River just outside. A backdrop of glorious Venice enriches the multinational flavor of the Haskell Free Library and Opera House (below), nestled in the midst of Rock-Island, Quebec, and Derby Line, Vermont. Here entertainers perform in Canada for the pleasure of an audience seated in the United States. Downstairs a six-room library serves both towns. Residents crossing the border to attend the theater or use the library need not go through customs. Both Quebec and Vermont register the 1904, Victorian-style landmark as a historic site.

*B*etween two worlds
and two nations,
young members of the
Mohawk nation witness
an ancestral ritual during
Akwesasne Friendship
Days, a yearly event
to foster cultural pride.
Their 18,000-acre St.
Regis reservation spreads
across the boundary into
Quebec, Ontario, and
New York; a toll bridge
on the St. Lawrence River
provides toll-free passage
for the Indians. Separate
tribal councils function
on each side of the border,
but many Mohawks here
regard their community
as a single nation, bound
by traditions older than
the dividing line drawn
by the United States
and Britain.

Through Inland Seas

From the Thousand Islands to Thunder Bay

I have just arrived in town—Alexandria Bay, New York—and some fellow is telling me that if I stick around for a few weeks I might become a million-aire. Organizers of a summer festival in the Thousand Islands are going to release a certain smallmouth bass, distinguished by a tag, into the St. Lawrence River. Catch that fish, this gent says eagerly, and you'll win yourself a check for $50,000 for each of the next 20 years.

Unfortunately, I couldn't wait for the debut of the prize fish. Yet by dint of the man's proposal I felt initiated into the spirit of things. What is a summer resort if not a place for fanciful dreams, especially a resort tagged Playground of Millionaires?

I had reached the threshold of the Great Lakes here in the Thousand Is-lands, a scenic archipelago that braids the upper St. Lawrence for 50 miles. The region marked a definite change of pace in my border journey. I had come from a month of visiting remote fishing and logging towns. Now suddenly I stepped into a vacationland. Splendid houses rose from the islands, and sleek boats packed the marinas. At night revelers promenaded through towns on shore. The Thousand Islands seemed a perfect setting for a million-dollar fish.

One bright June day I rented a small motorboat and joined a shoal of other craft out on the water. Speedboats and cabin cruisers raced back and forth like stampeding horses. Well out from shore I swung wide to avoid the path of an enormous cargo ship traveling the St. Lawrence Seaway, the international water route for Great Lakes commerce.

Soon a few islands appeared, their slopes thickly quilled with pines and hardwoods. Samuel de Champlain made a round guess when he named the Thousand Islands in 1615. The latest counts range up to 1,825 islands. Accord-ing to the local rules an island is an island only if two or more trees grow on it. Most of the islands are actually the tops of granite hills flooded 6,000 years ago by the river. I chose to weave around a few dozen of them, if only to appreciate the soaring Victorian manors with their towers and turrets, their verandas and gazebos—the backdrop, I imagined, for a Shaw play or Wodehouse story.

The wealthy—bankers, industrialists, heirs   *(Continued on page 64)*

Bound for seaports far from the sea, a 605-foot "laker" glides past an idle outboard in the Thousand Islands. Lakers haul cargoes only in the Great Lakes and St. Lawrence River—in contrast to "salties," freighters that ply the oceans as well as the inland seas.

oldt Castle, George Boldt's unfinished valentine to his wife, draws boatloads of tourists to heart-shaped Heart Island (below) on the New York side of the boundary. Work stopped on the 124-room dream house when Mrs. Boldt died in 1904. On the Ontario mainland St. Brandon's Church (opposite) beckons the faithful from the islands, its waterfront a parking lot for waterborne worshipers.

PRECEDING PAGES: *A saltie slowly threads the Thousand Islands past Alexandria Bay, New York. Dual roles of ship channel and pleasuring ground sometimes clash: Shippers want winter ice broken for year-round access, but islanders protest that ice floes in freighters' wakes threaten damage to boathouses and shorelines.*

Nature laid down the line through the Great Lakes, in days when treaty makers deemed a water route easier to define. They split four lakes down the middle—though Ben Franklin skewed the line northward in Superior to gain Isle Royale and its reported copper riches. Five states share the watery boundary with a single province, Ontario.

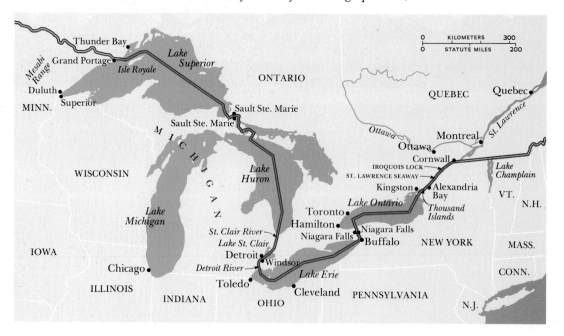

and heiresses—began flocking to the area in the late 1800s, with tennis rackets, fishing rods, parasols, and full evening dress packed in their steamer trunks. Yacht races enlivened the weekends. While the rich generally resorted to the islands, less affluent visitors boarded in sprawling riverside hotels, a pattern still followed today.

Every haunt of the wealthy, it seems, comes with a poignant tale; the islands are no exception. I circled Heart Island, where George Boldt, a hotel magnate and real estate operator in New York City and Philadelphia, envisioned a 124-room Rhineland castle as a present for his wife, Louise. In 1904, after he had re-shaped the island into a heart and spent two million dollars on construction, Louise died. Boldt never returned to the island, and his unfinished castle fell into disrepair. Since 1977 the 1000 Islands Bridge Authority has maintained Boldt Castle as a kind of Gothic-novel tourist attraction. It glows at night as if a banquet were in progress. But inside it is empty and cold, with the graffiti of thousands of names on the walls.

Like my path in the motorboat, the international border zigzags. Under terms of the Treaty of Ghent, which concluded the War of 1812, boundary commissioners agreed that no island would be divided. As they awarded islands to each side, the commissioners figured the credits and debits of the acreage involved. In the end, after marathon arguments and much compromise, their irregular line proved satisfactory to both sides.

Thinking about the border as I raced around, I noticed mostly motorboats on the American half of the river and sailboats on the Canadian side. In a funny way this symbolized some of the differences I had noticed in the people. My American compatriots tend to come on as more conspicuous and aggressive; Canadians appear more traditional and patient. Or so it seems to me.

One day I was invited to Club Island, which lies slightly south of the group that constitutes Canada's St. Lawrence Islands National Park. My hosts were the Haxalls from Riverdale, New York. Betty Haxall has spent more than 60 summers in the area; on this day she and her husband, Bolling, a retired newspaperman, had thrown open the windows of their roomy wooden cottage to air it out after the winter. What a wonderful place to spend the summer, I daydreamed: a shed full of boats, a porch shaded by century-old oaks, curtains lifted by a fresh river breeze. The Haxalls felt compelled to cite some of the inconveniences of island living: "We're at the beck and call of the weather. . . . We have constant trouble with the telephone wires. . . . There were mice in the linen closet and red squirrels in the stove." I barely heard them.

Later I stopped at a realty office in Alexandria Bay and asked what an island would cost. "Well, I have the House of the Seven Gables on Dashwood Island on the Canadian side," the agent said. "It has 23 rooms, 8 bathrooms, and costs $650,000." Including the island.

"I also have a couple of little islands with no heat or lights or indoor bathrooms. They go for twenty and up. Interested?" No, not really, I said. Not without a certain smallmouth bass in my possession.

From the point where the border leaves the 45th parallel and follows the St. Lawrence southward, it does not touch land for more than 1,700 miles—1,300 miles to where it departs from the Great Lakes, then another 400 miles of lake and stream until it reaches eastern Manitoba. This almost wasn't so. During the Treaty of Paris negotiations after the Revolutionary War, American representative John Jay proposed that the 45th parallel continue as the boundary all the way to the Mississippi River, the westernmost extent of the new nation. The United States would have gotten all of Lake Erie and Lake Ontario, and part of what is now the province of Ontario, including Toronto. To the British side would have fallen half of Minnesota, including the then undiscovered Mesabi iron range, as well as parts of Wisconsin and Michigan. The British balked, unwilling to yield the profitable fur-trading routes of the lower Great Lakes. Jay returned with a line-of-lakes proposal, the eventual boundary.

After skirting Lake Ontario on the Canadian side, I descended into the Niagara Peninsula, the site of bloody grapplings during the War of 1812. Rather than visit the battlegrounds, I shamelessly rushed to view one of North America's most famous tourist attractions, Niagara Falls. There it is: two broad curtains of blue-white water thundering down the rock wall, with hundreds of spectators lined above them, hurling superlatives into the spray.

Wedge-shaped Goat Island separates the cataract into the curving Horseshoe Falls, 173 feet high, on the Canadian side, and the taller—182 feet—but narrower American Falls with its high boulder-strewn base on the United States side. The latter includes Luna Falls. The tremendous flow represents the outpouring of four Great Lakes: Erie, Huron, Michigan, and Superior. This flood of water funnels down the 35-mile-long Niagara River and spills out over a high ledge to create the falls and the rapids and whirlpool below. I wondered if the merchants of tourism knew that scientists have predicted the eventual disappearance of the falls. They have already receded more than seven miles in the 12,000 years since they were formed at the end of the Ice Age. According to one set of theories the falls may back up all the way to Lake Erie in another 25,000 to 50,000 years, as water continues to erode the rock. A different theory notes that the Niagara River area is rising—rebounding in reaction to the disappearance of the ice sheets. In about 3,500 years, this theory goes, the river level will be higher than the level of Lake Erie. Under either process—erosion or rebound—the falls would disappear. There goes business.

The falls struck me as an old-fashioned and endearing spectacle. They're stuck between two aging cities and at night gaudy colored lights make them look like melting tutti-frutti. Yet our imaginations can never quite do justice to these mighty cascades. In the end we are left simply to stare, and marvel.

Niagara Falls, Ontario, lucked out over Niagara Falls, New York, for the best views. Thus the Canadian side is all dressed up with tall, revolving restaurants, Ferris wheels, and flashing neon lights. It looks like the midway of a state fair. Fast-food stands. Electronic-game arcades. Spook houses. Souvenir shops. The Elvis Presley museum. Niagara Falls, New York, bruised by a poor economy, looks stark and deserted by contrast.

Tradition says the mystique of a honeymoon mecca began when Napoleon's youngest brother brought his bride to the falls in the early 1800s. The reputation endures. Motels advertise prominently for newlyweds, offering two nights, a Jacuzzi, a water bed, and a bottle of champagne at a package price. I stood at a greeting booth for an hour and met 18 couples who came to pick up the honeymooners' certificate offered by the visitor bureau on the Canadian side. Most of the newlyweds were in their 20s and somewhat shy. About half said their parents had come here for their honeymoons.

The great rush of water, I heard it said, may work in some mysterious way to enhance romantic feelings. However that may be, the water in the Niagara River has surely fostered a special relationship between the United States and Canada. A 1950 treaty specifies that the two countries must always allow a certain amount of water to run over the falls to preserve the scenic splendor: a daytime flow of 100,000 cubic feet per second during the prime tourist season from April to October, 50,000 at night and during the off-season. As for the rest of the flow—often more than half—the two countries divide it, diverting it through large tunnels to massive hydroelectric plants below the rapids. The Sir Adam Beck complex at Queenston, Ontario, and the Robert Moses plant in Lewiston, New York, combine to generate nearly four million kilowatts—enough to light up a city the size of Chicago.

One modern note—a discordant one—intrudes to spoil blithe contemplation of the falls. The water that plunges so majestically over the precipice carries with it industrial wastes. Besides runoff of pesticides and discharges of heavy metals such as chromium and mercury, toxic substances such as dioxin are seeping from a few dozen of the 164 chemical dumps in the area. The hazardous-waste sites include the infamous Love Canal in Niagara Falls, New York, where a neighborhood has been abandoned. The Niagara River provides drinking

Sounding its own thunder, building its own clouds, Niagara Falls storms into the maelstrom. Maid of the Mist, laden with sightseers, churns past American and Luna Falls (at right); beyond Goat Island (far right) spreads Horseshoe Falls. The flow down Niagara's cataracts varies from 50,000 to 100,000 cubic feet per second.

water for 400,000 people. Though public officials assure local inhabitants that the water quality remains safe, Americans and Canadians continue to demand an accelerated cleanup of all sources of potential hazard.

The motley history of Niagara Falls is incomplete without mention of the exhibitionism that the place inspires. Two museums on the Ontario side feature barrels, tubes, rubber balls, and other contraptions used by daredevils who have plunged down the falls or ridden the ferocious rapids. Only six people have survived a descent, including a seven-year-old boy protected by nothing more than a life vest when he fell from a boat and was swept over the falls. Shortly before I arrived, a Canadian power company employee dived into the river with a safety line around his waist to rescue a young American woman floundering near the brink. In July 1984 a professional stuntman safely—though illegally—took the plunge in a barrel made of steel and plastic. He was fined $500.

" 'After God you have the Master.' That's the saying. No one else on board can say 'do this' or 'do that.' " Captain Christian Collée, Belgian shipmaster, thus summed up his authority aboard the 730-foot *Federal Danube*, carrying imported steel to the Great Lakes. As Captain Collée gave orders in English inside the spacious pilothouse, five stories above the deck, a tugboat pushed the bright red ship away from its mooring in Montreal harbor. Next stop: Toronto.

I had backtracked to Montreal—somewhat beyond the range of my border transit—to take passage through the St. Lawrence Seaway, a segment of the St. Lawrence-Great Lakes system. Paralleling the border for a good part of its length, the system stretches 2,342 miles from the Atlantic Ocean to Duluth, Minnesota, on Lake Superior. A network of rivers, lakes, and canals, the waterway has been hailed for creating a "fourth coast" on the continent.

Two weeks out of Antwerp, the *Federal Danube* slowly moved out into Montreal harbor. On the bridge, preparing to take the ship through the first set of locks, stood a river pilot, required on all oceangoing vessels on the Seaway.

French explorer Jacques Cartier sailed this way in 1535 as he probed for a northwest passage to the Orient. Just upstream he was turned back by rapids. A century later these rapids were named Lachine—for China—in mocking reference to the dream of a northwest passage by another French explorer, the Sieur de La Salle. Lachine Rapids are the first in a hazardous series that makes the upper St. Lawrence unnavigable for much of the 180 miles between Montreal and Lake Ontario. Over time locks and canals were built to provide access to the lakes. One of the most ambitious projects, the construction of the Erie Canal between Buffalo, New York, and the Hudson River in the early 1800s, made Buffalo the first major port on the Great Lakes.

None of the bypasses were deep enough for oceangoing ships until the Seaway opened in 1959. Its streamlined system of three canals and seven locks on the upper river replaced a bottleneck of some 20 locks. With channels and locks dug to a 27-foot depth, transoceanic commercial ships could for the first time sail into the industrial and agricultural heart of the continent.

In addition to the Seaway the St. Lawrence-Great Lakes system includes an eight-lock staircase in the Welland Canal, an engineering marvel that detours ships around Niagara Falls and overcomes the 326-foot drop from Lake Erie to Lake Ontario. To complete the system, locks at Sault Ste. Marie bypass the river rapids between Lakes Huron and Superior. In all, this network on the inland seas raises and lowers ships 557 feet, the largest such operation in the world.

No entry into a lock is routine; an accident can stall Seaway traffic and perhaps tear a hole in a ship. At St-Lambert near Montreal the 80-foot-wide berth allowed the *Federal Danube* only two feet of clearance on either side. "Starboard ten," pilot Florian Boudreault called out. "Starboard ten," the helmsman repeated, moving the rudder ten degrees to swing the ship to the right. "Steady," the pilot said, peering at a compass and then walking quickly with the captain to look over the side as the lock walls came closer. "Midships, port five." The bow of the ship straightened. "Dead slow." The huge ship slid snugly into the lock. "Congratulations," I called. The pilot turned and said, "It's a job."

For ten minutes more than 20 million gallons of gravity-fed water spilled into the enclosed lock. Almost imperceptibly the ship rose 15 feet. Then the gates opened and the *Federal Danube,* with a boom of its whistle, sailed out of

Mary and Winston Greaves sort handpicked pie cherries in southern Ontario's fertile fruit belt, an area that remembers the distant days of turbulence along the border. American troops, surging across the Niagara River in 1813, overran Newark—today's town of Niagara-on-the-Lake—and Fort George, and left them in flames.

*B*right, growing, fresh-faced,
Toronto the New banishes the
image of old Toronto the Good, dozing
primly along Lake Ontario. Pleasure
craft jam the city's marinas, cargo
carriers crowd its port. A striking
status symbol punctuates the skyline:
1,815-foot CN Tower, the world's tallest
freestanding structure. At Ontario
Place, a waterfront playground on
man-made islets, the Cinesphere shows
films on a six-story screen. Diners
and strollers enjoy a summer day
in downtown's refurbished Yorkville
(below left). Ethnic styles flourish;
a shopper (below) scans the racks in
the street bazaar of Kensington Market.
Toronto's name seems to have been
derived from a Huron term for "a place
of meeting." With official encouragement
Canada's immigrants may choose to
think of their new home as a meeting
place rather than a melting pot.

Montreal harbor. An hour later we were lifted 30 feet at the Côte-Ste-Catherine locks, leaving the Lachine Rapids behind.

Captain Collée stayed up all night. In his white shirt with gold trim and epaulets the master stalked the pilothouse, smoking a cigar to stay awake. "Everything has to go very fast now," he mused. "We were in Montreal for only two days. When I started out 15 years ago, we would stay 15 days in port. But look at the cost of running a vessel. It's anywhere from $3,000 to $15,000 a day, depending on the size of the crew." Shipboard life has changed also. "A ship is more like an anonymous big-city apartment now," Collée said. "Before the days of air conditioning and single compartments, the crew would come out on deck in the evening to talk and drink beer. Now the hallways are quiet and everyone is inside his own apartment."

Around noon the next day we passed through the Iroquois lock on the Canadian side of the river—the last lock on the Seaway. From the west a rusty Soviet ship, the *Kapitan Sviridov*, passed us, followed by the Austrian *Traun*. In 1982 some 4,300 vessels from more than 30 nations threaded the Seaway with a total of 43 million metric tons of cargo, principally grain and iron ore. The *Federal Danube* was carrying 18,000 tons, most of it steel bars, coils, and structural parts, plus some combines and automobiles. She could have carried 26,000 tons before reaching the maximum draft for the waterway—26 feet. After planned delivery stops in Toronto, Cleveland, and Toledo, the ship would call at Duluth, hoping to take on grain. The round-trip from Europe would take six weeks. For the cargoes she carried, Seaway tolls and pilotage costs would total $25,000.

Recession in the steel industry and competition from Atlantic seaports and from truck and barge routes along the Mississippi River have cut into Seaway traffic. Captain Collée remarked that some pilots bitterly complain to him when they learn he is hauling imported steel while thousands of North American steelworkers go without jobs. "I just keep quiet," he told me. "The foreign steel is cheaper. Besides, I'm not responsible for the type of load. I'll carry a ship full of manure if I'm asked." Less than a month after we spoke the United States imposed tight quotas on specialty steel coming into the country.

Traveling through the Thousand Islands, right on the border, the ship flew three flags—the Canadian, U.S., and Belgian. Proposals to open the Seaway to winter navigation—it currently operates from April to freeze-up in December—run into heated opposition here. Residents complain that the work required to keep an open channel could result in eroded shorelines, damaged boathouses and docks, and disturbed wildlife habitat. Conscious of the effect of her wake, the *Federal Danube* crawled along at nine knots. Speed limits are strictly enforced on the Seaway; a ticket costs $1,000.

Familiar islands passed below me. From a hundred feet up the cabin cruisers looked puny. Even some of the mansions appeared humble in size. My mood had changed in the ten days since I visited the islands. Then I luxuriated

Bells of the old City Hall clock tower first sounded at the moment the 20th century arrived in Toronto—81 years before the 36-story Cadillac Fairview office tower opened. Its mirror skin reflects the sky. The downtown boom roused fears of overcrowding and years of soul-searching as the city sought to build livability into future growth.

in the slow time of a summer resort. Now I eagerly anticipated the crowds and big-city hum of Toronto and Detroit coming up on the border.

Thirty-five hours after leaving Montreal, the *Federal Danube* pulled into the port of Toronto on Lake Ontario. I bade farewell to Captain Collée and soon was swallowed by the city. The largest city in the country with a metropolitan population of three million—it surpassed Montreal in the late '70s—Toronto is charged like a magnet. It has attracted a quarter of all recent immigrants to Canada, the head offices of many of Canada's leading corporations, and a concentration of artists and impresarios that helps rank Toronto high among North American cities in the number of cultural offerings. For an eastern metropolis it possesses the well-scrubbed and optimistic air of a western city. As Jane Jacobs, a prominent student of cities, said after moving from New York to Toronto in the late 1960s: "Here is the most hopeful and healthy city in North America, still unmangled, still with options."

For five days I sampled the life of Canada's proud centerpiece. I joined the ceaseless tide on Yonge Street (pronounced *young*), where spiky-haired New Wavers and arcade hangers-on mingled with soldiers of commerce with their attaché cases and brisk strides, and with young professional couples, boutique shopping bags swinging from their arms. Success and wealth gleam in gold at the new district headquarters of the Royal Bank of Canada; a quarter of a million dollars' worth of gold flakes tint its glass walls. Capital of Canada's richest and most populous province, strategically located on the Great Lakes trade route, Toronto has evolved into the financial seat of the country.

One day I rode up the CN Tower, Toronto's concrete needle in the sky. At 1,815 feet the Canadian National Railways communications tower is the world's tallest freestanding structure. Local wags say the revolving restaurant goes round once every 60 dollars. The city sparkles below ground as well—with a four-mile network of downtown shopping malls and pedestrian walkways. In this stylish burrow—built in deference to the Canadian winters—one can shop, eat, work, and exercise without stepping outdoors.

The city also has no visible slums; but its greatest distinction is its aura of safety. Metropolitan Toronto police in 1982 recorded 44 homicides, compared to 515 in Detroit. What a rare, nearly extinct feeling it is to walk anywhere in a large, multicultural city without fear.

As recently as 30 years ago Toronto was apparently one cold, gray morning of a city. Toronto the Good it was called, a dull regional center dominated by citizens of British stock. What caused the vibrant transformation? "It was the immigrants," declared Eva Allmen of Ontario Welcome House, a service center for new immigrants and refugees. "I came from South America in the early 1950s and this city is very different now." Change began shortly after her arrival, she said, with the influx of large numbers of Italians. The most dramatic gain in sophistication, she added, came with the Hungarian refugees in 1956. Hungary's attempt to turn away from Communism had been suppressed, and people fled to freer lands. "That's when the cafes and boutiques started to appear in Toronto," she recalled.

Liberalized immigration laws in Canada after World War II drew a worldwide response. People from more than 80 ethnic groups live in Toronto today;

about 40 percent of the population has origins other than British or French. Toronto's Italian, Portuguese, and Chinese communities represent some of the largest concentrations of those nationalities outside the home country. "When Italy won the World Cup in soccer in 1982," one resident told me, "this place was a riot of red, white, and green streamers."

Witness the piquant mix in Kensington Market, near the University of Toronto: In a two-block area I saw a Greek butcher, his cages of ducks, chickens, and rabbits cluttering the sidewalk; a Ukrainian billiard parlor; a Thai hardware store; a Portuguese grocer; a West Indian record shop with men in dreadlocks outside; and a Chinese seafood market. All that seemed to be missing was an American hamburger joint.

In absorbing immigrants Canadians like to say they are creating a mosaic, as opposed to a melting pot. Instead of promoting assimilation, government programs, especially in the schools, are encouraging immigrants to keep alive their foreign heritage.

"I think Canada's balancing act between the English and the French created an atmosphere that supports retention of an ethnic identity and is not conducive to assimilation," reflected Morris Diakowsky, an official in the Ontario Ministry of Citizenship and Culture. "But only so much is possible. People have to accept that you can't live as an Italian in Toronto as you could in Rome. We are all Canadians."

Toronto the New has enlisted a legion of protectors, especially in preserving the livability of downtown. Citizens' groups have effectively fought expressways and high-rise developments. The intense concern for the quality of life even had city officials auditioning musicians before permitting them to play in subway stations.

In a city whose population has more than doubled in 30 years, civic leaders see their main challenge as keeping the city manageable and dynamic at once. The strategy includes both rigorous zoning laws and ambitious projects. In the office of Stephen McLaughlin, head of the Department of Planning and Development, I looked over drawings for the waterfront, a plan to turn the city's face back toward Lake Ontario. The billion-dollar, 20-year project would replace a tangle of railroad tracks with parks, streets, office buildings, thousands of new housing units, and recreation and cultural centers. "The idea of a 24-hour city is very important to us," McLaughlin said, nodding his head in satisfaction.

The city planning office, I found, includes one person assigned solely to entertaining Americans who, according to McLaughlin, "come in and say, 'How do you do it?' " Of course, Toronto's not perfect. Racial tensions do exist. People complain of exorbitant housing costs. And Montrealers insist that their city remains livelier and more sophisticated. "I think Toronto is in its young adulthood as a world-class city," the distinguished Canadian novelist Robertson Davies said of his home. "It doesn't have the richness and cultivation yet. But its intimacy has kept us from the rot of cities where a tremendous center is deserted at night—except for figures lurking in the shadows."

To the southwest the border metropolis of Detroit teeters between two very

And they're off! Workhorses of the waterways jockey for position in the annual Freedom Festival Tugboat Race on the Detroit River. Averaging 13 knots, the winner sprinted the four-mile course in less than 14 minutes. The river, a boundary route, separates Detroit (its skyline rising in the distance) from Windsor, Ontario (at right).

different versions of the future: one as a barren and decayed industrial city beset by crime, poverty, and despair; the other as a reborn center of commerce and services, radiating energy and promise. Powerful downward tugs have pulled at Detroit in recent years. When economic recession spread across the nation in the early 1980s, Detroit, in the eyes of its leaders, suffered a full-scale depression. At the time of my visit a third of the city's 1.2 million people were receiving public assistance of some kind; soup kitchens were feeding 20,000 people a day. Large areas of the city had become ugly, dangerous slums. The auto industry, backbone of the economy, had been through a four-year slump.

Despite all, Detroit manages to display signs of revival. The waterfront on the Detroit River, once a grubby warehouse district, today features a glittery office complex, a large public plaza, and an auditorium and sports arena. The city is establishing itself as a major convention center (it hosted the Republican national convention in 1980). People are beginning to move back downtown. Some neighborhoods are being restored. Ethnic festivals are drawing large crowds. Community leaders talk spiritedly about the "comeback city."

The waterfront was jammed during my stay. Detroit and Windsor—the quiet, well-preserved sister city of 200,000 across the river in Ontario—were throwing a ten-day bash in celebration of Canada Day, July 1, and Independence Day, July 4. The festivities on the U.S. side took place where Antoine Laumet de la Mothe Cadillac, a French soldier, established a strategic trading post in 1701. Cadillac called his post Fort Pontchartrain du Détroit—Fort

Pontchartrain of the Strait—referring to the stream that links Lake Erie and Lake St. Clair. Today the strait is known as the Detroit River.

Thousands of people poured into Hart Plaza to see jugglers, skydivers, military bands, and a pop group whose rendition of "Dancing in the Streets" revved up the crowd. The people came from the inner city and the outer city, from affluent suburbs like Grosse Pointe, and from across the river in Canada. Youngsters arrived in cap and gown, fresh from high school graduation ceremonies; some wore their mortarboards at jaunty angles.

"You'd be surprised at the high morale," insisted Coleman Young, Detroit's first black mayor, serving his third term. "It stems from Detroit being a blue-collar city. These people are used to economic vicissitudes. We've survived the Great Depression, and we're surviving what we call the Second Great Depression. Detroit has been the hardest hit of any city over one million. But look around you, there's evidence of confidence and preparation for the future. Look at the new buildings."

A visitor can not help noticing the Renaissance Center. This futuristic sextet of tall, glass-sheathed buildings rises from the riverbank like the capitol of Oz. The RenCen was the brainstorm of Henry Ford II, grandson of the auto industry legend. Determined to see Detroit revitalized after the devastating racial riots of 1967, Henry Ford II, then chairman of the Ford Motor Company, persuaded 50 other local companies to join in building a dazzling hotel and office center on the river. At a cost of 350 million dollars it was one of the largest privately financed real estate developments in urban history. The RenCen joined the skyline in 1977, just as the rumbles of a worldwide recession began to jar the already battered city. (Between 1970 and 1980 Detroit lost 182 manufacturing plants, 30,000 jobs, and 300,000 people.) Plagued by a lack of customers, RenCen has lost money steadily, the total in six years equaling a fifth of the original cost.

Yet by most accounts the RenCen has succeeded as a symbol, bringing an emotional lift to the hard-pressed citizenry. It has also served as a catalyst, spurring other new development downtown. "If we hadn't built the place, people would have viewed Detroit as a tired old city where nothing is happening," said Robert McCabe, president of Detroit Renaissance, an organization of business leaders. "Detroit was a city without a center. Now that we have recaptured the waterfront, we are starting to establish a new identity for the city. And remember, the Detroit River is one of the few things the suburbs can't steal from us."

The most noted positive thinker is Mayor Young himself. "When you review our blessings—and you search desperately for them at times like this—you have to look at the fresh water all around us," the mayor said, glancing at the river outside his office window. "That is our asset; that is what will guarantee our progress." The Great Lakes, he noted, contain the major proportion of the nation's fresh surface water and a fifth of the world's. *(Continued on page 84)*

FOLLOWING PAGES: Fiery flowers bloom as Detroit and Windsor join in their annual tribute to freedom and friendship. With parades, exhibitions, and concerts, the festival spans two national holidays: the U.S. Independence Day observance on July 4 and Canada Day, commemorating the creation of the Dominion on July 1, 1867. Behind the fireworks Detroit's new skyscrapers glow with the promise of the Renaissance City.

railer load of Detroit's bread-and-butter product rolls toward Windsor on the Ambassador Bridge, the longest suspension span between two countries. Some 12 million travelers use the bridge and a nearby tunnel each year, making Detroit-Windsor the busiest corridor on the border. Here the lay of the land reverses the normal traffic flow: U.S.-bound motorists drive north; Canada lies to the south. A view from the bridge captures a pair of leapers defying gravity in a Detroit pickup game (below). Stop, go, dribble, pass, block, dunk, one-on-one—in playground basketball city youngsters endure the long testing that sends the best of them to college teams, TV fame, and the pros.

FOLLOWING PAGES: No longer a reeking industrial sewer, the Detroit River once more lures fishermen to its shores. The cleanup, begun in the 1960s, paralleled a broad rejuvenation of the Great Lakes waters—though scientists still find contamination in fishes. A 31-mile strait, or détroit, the Detroit River runs from Lake St. Clair to Lake Erie, but rare wind conditions may raise Erie's water level enough to reverse the flow.

Though plentiful fresh water may represent hope for the future, the success of Motor City still hinges on the auto industry. In the metropolitan area one out of every ten jobs depends on that industry. Imports and a weak economy brought domestic new-car sales from a record ten million in 1973 to roughly half that amount in 1982. Substantial layoffs sent shock waves through Detroit. With the rebound in 1983 unemployment in the motor vehicle sector was reduced by more than half. And as auto sales continued strong into 1984, industry profit figures made rosy headlines.

Most of the assembly plants were closed during my July visit as the industry retooled for the next year's models. At the 60-year-old Clark Street plant, however, Cadillacs were still rolling out. The line rarely stopped moving. Gas tanks, bumpers, engines, and hoods floated through the air on a feeder line. On the main line the workers quickly bolted, screwed, and clamped on the parts. Each worker has approximately one minute per job. A woman read a newspaper, a couple of paragraphs at a time, between charging batteries. Engineers and foremen, in white shirts and ties, roamed the line.

From the time a dark metal chassis drops down on the line to when a Cadillac rolls off, about three hours pass. Fifty cars come off the line every hour, 800 a day. On each, someone slaps a sticker reading, "American Made by Americans Who Care."

During my stay in Detroit, Mayor Young ordered a curfew on youths under 18, in response to a rash of violent crimes. A few days later a more positive news item surfaced. In the gymnasium of Murray Wright High School the mayor honored four female Junior Police Cadets for saving the life of a girl, a victim in a knife attack. Another example, I noted, of Detroit traveling that wobbly line between despair and hope.

Driving back from the high school, I passed through a slum. I barely had the heart to look at the vacant lots glinting with broken glass, the shabby houses with sagging porches, the groups of men standing listlessly on street corners. My mood sank, but I was quickly admonished by the marquee of an abandoned movie theater. It read: "Say Something Nice About Detroit."

The carnival taking place in Detroit and Windsor made it hard to conjure up the time when British and American troops faced off across the strait. Detroit fell to the British early in the War of 1812. But it was retaken a year later, after a fleet under Oliver Hazard Perry defeated the British on Lake Erie.

Since large fighting ships in those days could not sail into the inland seas, they were built right on the lakes—though the Royal Navy sent supplies, including freshwater casks to ships floating in fresh water. In 1814 Kingston, Ontario, launched the 112-gun *St. Lawrence,* largest of all Canada-built ships until 1945. Peace arrived before the Americans could complete the even bigger *New Orleans* across Lake Ontario at Sackets Harbor, New York. There the unfinished giant sat for nearly 70 years, until she was sold for scrap.

The war's end led to the Rush-Bagot Agreement of 1817, a milestone of diplomacy. The two rivals agreed to limit themselves to four armed vessels each on the entire Great Lakes and Lake Champlain. Though slightly modified, the agreement still stands. Shortly before World War II the United States needed Canada's permission to conduct naval exercises on the lakes. The lakeland

*From birchbarks to behemoths: After nearly 200 years the Soo Canals still hold the key to escaping the rapids—*sault*—of the St. Marys River. Westbound from Lake Huron, the* Columbia Star, *1,000 feet long and 105 feet wide, squeezes into the Poe Lock for a 20-foot lift to Lake Superior. Sault Ste. Marie, Ontario, stretches along the riverside.*

border has produced a number of other significant pacts. The Boundary Waters Treaty of 1909 created the International Joint Commission, which investigates disagreements arising from the use of water along the frontier and proposes solutions. And the Great Lakes Water Quality Agreement, first signed in 1972, commits both nations to safeguarding the environment of the basin that supplies drinking water to 20 million Canadians and Americans. Joint action has also successfully waged war on the sea lamprey, a primitive form of predator fish that nearly ruined the commercial fishery on the lakes. In recent years the two countries have been trying to counter the latest threat to the fisheries—toxic chemicals including such substances as PCBs.

From Detroit I flew to the twin cities of Sault Ste. Marie, Ontario, and Sault Ste. Marie, Michigan. Between them frothed the *sault* named for St. Mary by French missionaries. The rushing water must have provided appropriate ceremonial thunder in 1671 when French soldiers and priests met with delegates of 14 Indian tribes and proclaimed that the interior of North America now belonged to King Louis XIV. Since that time the rapids have been whittled in half by the construction of a power canal for a hydroelectric plant.

The sault of St. Mary posed the last natural obstacle in the Great Lakes waterway. To sidestep the 20-foot white water drop between Lakes Superior and Huron a lock for canoes was first built in 1797. Today, Poe Lock, one of four parallel locks on the American side, accommodates 1,000-foot-long ore ships, a dozen of which ply the Great Lakes.

One day I joined a string of spectators on the American side of the Soo to watch the gigantic cargo ships shoehorn in and out of the long, narrow locks. Through them moves about two-thirds of all the iron ore produced in the two countries. Across the river in Canada large white feathers of smoke rose from a

Outcasts of Ice Age glaciers, granitic cobbles (opposite) pave the beach at Gargantua Harbour, long a haven for Indians, fur traders, and fishermen. Today it serves campers along a rugged coastal trail in Lake Superior Provincial Park. At Thunder Bay stands a monument to courage, larger than life. In 1980 Terry Fox, a 22-year-old amputee, began a cross-Canada Marathon of Hope; 3,339 miles later he faltered near here—the run cut short, but not the hope: 24 million dollars poured in for cancer research.

FOLLOWING PAGES: Windsurfers share the dawn's early light with an ore carrier bound for Thunder Bay—half a continent from the sea, yet Canada's second port in bulk tonnage. Indian legend tells how the Sleeping Giant and the Thunderbird brewed a great storm, vainly struggling to keep white men from a treasure island in Thunder Bay.

blast furnace of the Algoma Steel Corporation; its docks were laden with dunes of iron ore pellets, coal, and limestone. Behind me in Michigan lay Portage Avenue with a faceless collection of hotels and restaurants. More than a century ago, before the first large locks were built, teams of mules and oxen tramped this route, dragging vessels over greased skids. This detour could take three months. Today a ship floats through the locks in less than half an hour.

It was an impersonal spectacle along the locks until I noticed the woman staring intently down the lake. Mary Igercich said her son Steve, a crewman on a laker, was scheduled to come through the locks from Lake Superior. Mary, who lived in Sault Ste. Marie, Ontario, hoped his ship would use MacArthur Lock, the closest to shore, so she could talk to Steve for a few moments while his ship slowly lowered to the level of Lake Huron.

Soon she called out, "There's his ship." Mary stared quietly as the 608-foot *Mantadoc*, laden with grain, slid into Poe Lock—too far away for a talk. A young man in a blue T-shirt and yellow hard hat stood on the deck and waved. Mary, her body straining forward against the railing, waved back, all her words of concern and affection caged in her mouth.

The *Mantadoc* had come from Thunder Bay, Ontario, on the northwestern shore of Superior. Like Toronto and Detroit, the city of Thunder Bay had its roots in the fur trade, having been formed from Port Arthur and Fort William.

The lake port still depends upon goods brought from the interior of Canada, but instead of fur pelts piled high in canoes, the valuable cargo today comes in the form of boxcars stuffed with grain. Enormous grain terminals ring the harbor. More than 17 million tons of wheat, oats, barley, and rapeseed annually

leave Thunder Bay by rail or ship, making it the world's largest grain-handling port. In bulk tonnage it is Canada's leading port after Vancouver.

I took a tour of the harbor and saw the *Ralph Misener* pulled up alongside the Saskatchewan Wheat Pool 7 terminal, a golden flood of wheat pouring from a hose into her hold. It would take 11 hours to fill the ship. "The *Ralph Misener* can hold one million bushels," the guide proudly informed us. "That's the equivalent of what's grown on a 51,000-acre farm."

Industry had a way of showing off in the Great Lakes, I thought, mostly through its proud statistics: the amount of grain that can fill a ship, or the number of cars that roll off an assembly line, or what size city could be lit by the kilowatts generated by a hydroelectric plant.

I also remembered the idle ships, the cold blast furnaces, the closed shops, and the lines of the poor waiting for hot soup. The boom and bust of two nations come into focus along their water border. What kept surprising me, though, was that many of the people I met, from young honeymooners to the mayor of a troubled city, all talked big, optimistic about the next day, or the next year, or the next century. Of course someone can catch a million-dollar fish reads the message on the border. The guide's voice cut in: "The terminal in front of you collapsed on its pilings in 1959. But as you see, it's been rebuilt. It holds 8.25 million bushels. That's. . . ."

By Paddle
and Portage

From the Boundary Waters to the Northwest Angle

Picture the setting: Two canoes alone on an expanse of water. Two million acres of lakes and woods surround them. A leaden sky is breaking up, and shafts of sunlight pierce the wall of pines and firs on shore. No sound except the rhythmic dip of paddles. Everything seems perfect and in place—except for the strange geometry of a large sign ahead. The boats glide closer and a laugh rings out as we read: Please Report To Customs.

Even here in the spacious canoe wilderness along the Minnesota-Ontario line the business of national sovereignty goes on. We unloaded the gear, and the two guides—Stu Osthoff and Randy Skube—hefted the 70-pound canoes bottom up onto their broad shoulders, assuming the headless pose of portagers. Photographer Mike Yamashita, his friend Woolsey James from New Jersey, and I slung onto our backs large canvas bags called Duluth packs. In single file on an August morning we trod the foot-beaten path of Prairie Portage, from Sucker Lake to Basswood Lake and Canada.

At the end of the trail we came upon a small white cottage. In a domesticated yard sat a lawn mower near a flagpole flapping the Maple Leaf of Canada. Agent Gordon Matheson, looking official and uncomfortably warm in his uniform, put us through the formalities. He asked what country we were citizens of. He told us we were allowed two days' food free of duty; after that the cost per person was $1.40 Canadian ($1.12 U.S.) a day. For camping permits and fishing licenses, he said, we must walk a hundred yards to the park ranger's cottage.

It seemed to me that the sovereignty of the two nations might well survive without a customs port here in the wilderness. "No station here!" Agent Matheson said incredulously when I suggested the possibility. "If this was made a free port, it would be abused sooner or later."

The U.S. customs station was back near Ely, Minnesota, 20 miles to the southwest, where we had begun our six-day dabble in the lake country. South of the border we paddled the Boundary Waters Canoe Area Wilderness (BWCAW), a million-acre piece of protected wilderness inside the Superior National Forest. Stretching 150 miles along the international boundary, the BWCAW is part of a larger region pockmarked with thousands *(Continued on page 96)*

Along a route the voyageurs knew, wilderness paddlers reload canoes after portaging Basswood River rapids. Before the arrival of railroads, travelers depended on the sprawling web of border lakes and streams for inland transportation.

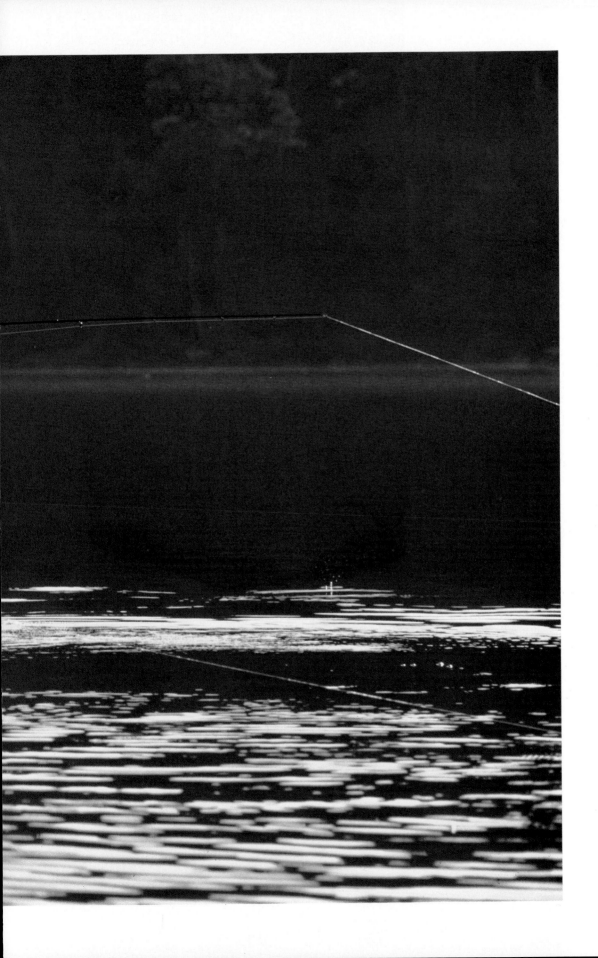

"*Cedar water*"—tinted by decomposing bark and needles—foams past glacier-hewn granite of Curtain Falls. Ice Age glaciers, says a local biologist, "were ruthless on this country, left us with little soil, lots of boulders . . . and thousands of nice lakes." Portaging between the waters has grown easier with time. Voyageurs hefted wooden boats of more than 200 pounds; today a portager (below) balances 70 pounds of plastic. At the Prairie Portage border crossing (below right) Canada posts a warning against smuggling.

PRECEDING PAGES: Trolling anglers rely on steady paddling—rather than the motor—to keep a taut line. Canadian and U.S. wilderness rules forbid the use of motors on most lakes in the area.

From Lake Superior to Manitoba an old voyageurs' highway continues the boundary through lakes and rivers—not all navigable. Canoemen faced a nine-mile carry from Grand Portage. Before agreeing to this border, the U.S. had sought the northern line beginning near Thunder Bay, while Britain claimed the land south to Duluth.

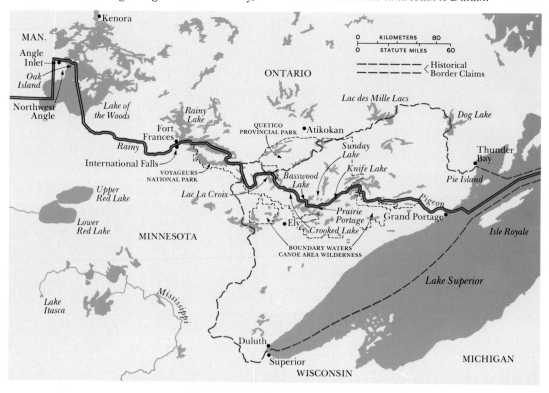

of lakes, the aftermath of glaciers advancing and retreating. Almost 200,000 people come here each year to fish and canoe, in a setting that looks much as it did when French-Canadian voyageurs traversed the lakes with their bundles of pelts and trade goods two centuries ago.

North of the line Quetico Provincial Park spreads across another million acres of water and rocky shores. It is a less crowded wilderness (40,000 annual visitors) due to slightly tighter entry quotas and greater distances from population centers. Use of motors is banned in Quetico and in most of the Boundary Waters as well. Logging ended in both areas in the 1970s.

To spend a night in this section of Quetico can require as much advance planning as reserving a seat for a popular Broadway play. Because of the threat of overuse, overnight permits are issued to only 15 groups a day entering from the U.S. side at Prairie Portage. Usually, by the middle of May, quotas for most of the summer have been filled.

Cleared to enter, we paddled about three miles up Basswood, then four miles up Sunday Lake. In the Quetico-Superior country canoeing usually amounts to long, straight-ahead hauls. The scenery is more serene than spectacular—blue sheets of water, unbroken palisades of trees, cloud-rent skies. Gritty satisfaction comes from cutting precise strokes of the paddle, hearing the whoosh of the canoe splitting the chop, huffing and puffing on portages, and after all these exertions, making camp at a spot where there is no one else.

The voyageurs—sitting six to ten in their 25-foot-long birchbark *canots du nord*—took a break about every hour in their sprints across the water. For ten minutes they puffed on long-stemmed pipes, then back to the paddles, often singing to keep time to the strokes or for the pleasure of the *bourgeois,* the boss. They calculated the length of lakes in *pipes,* or the number of breaks required for a crossing. After paddling about three pipes, we reached our reward: unattended Louisa Falls, where water toppled off a cliff into a sun-warmed bowl. Like liberated Boy Scouts, we shed our clothes and splashed in.

Back in the canoes we silenced our chatter when we heard a loon cry loudly on the lake. Even at close quarters that wild cry can sound like a distant wail. We looked around and saw a common loon swimming 30 yards from us. Suddenly, the black-headed bird plunked itself underwater. Clumsy on land, the loon is a powerful underwater swimmer and a skillful fisher. It dives easily to 30 feet, and in times of stress can stay below for three minutes.

Short of a minute the bird popped up and again uttered its eerie, stirring cry. For all the bears, moose, foxes, wolves, and other dramatic creatures in the region, it is the plain, often seen, often heard loon that strikes the most sensitive chord. Perhaps this is because the loon's wails and yodels intensify the feeling of solitude on these remote lakes. Sometimes a pair of loons will claim an entire small lake for themselves and their young—seeking to bar others of their kind from the breeding territory. I empathize with the loons' desire to be left alone. After all, why did we paddle half the day to this waterfall?

In Ely people had told me about a 76-year-old woman who evidently prefers seasons of solitude. We found her one day on an island in Knife Lake, on the U.S. side. White-haired Dorothy Molter sat by a stove inside a large wall tent cluttered with fishing rods, bunk beds, coffee cans, and gas lanterns. The first thing I could think to ask was, "Are you a hermit?"

Dorothy thrust at me an old copy of the *Saturday Evening Post,* its pages turned to a story entitled "Loneliest Woman in America." The story was about her. "When I saw that title," Dorothy said in her deep voice, "I could have fallen through the floor."

As it turns out, as many as 7,000 people drop in on her during the summer. Dorothy—the resident human—is a celebrity in the BWCAW. From her funky outpost she sells homemade root beer and a dozen kinds of candy bars to whoever shows up. "I never came here to get away from people," she said. "I like to see people, but thank goodness summer lasts only a few months."

Dorothy has lived here year round since the 1940s, when she moved from Chicago to nurse the ailing owner of a fishing camp. Inheriting the property when the owner died, Dorothy stayed on alone, heading into Ely a few times a year for supplies, cutting her own ice and wood, shooting grouse for meat, scaring bears away at night. When she decided to make a little money by selling soft drinks to thirsty canoeists, her place quickly became a popular stop. In 1966 the United States Forest Service bought her property; but as a forest volunteer Dorothy can remain for the rest of her life. Friends and Forest Service people bring out her supplies now and help with chores. Every summer morning, however, Dorothy is up early boiling water for root beer.

Outside the tent at an icebox she watched a dozen youngsters gulping root beer and downing chocolate bars. Years of labor have put a stoop in her posture, but she still looks hale and strong. "When I came up here I had no idea things would end up like this," she said, glancing around the island. In a few months, at freeze-up, she would retreat willingly to her log cabin for a winter of reading old newspapers and working on a scrapbook of bird feathers.

For our six-day outing I figured we made more than 30 portages, not counting the few times we had to drag the canoes over beaver dams. No one looked particularly thrilled on these tramps up and down rocky paths, straining under packs and canoes. One portage—Horse—was a mile long. Even the voyageurs, known for their stamina and strength, cursed the portages. They packed on their backs two or three 90-pound bales at a time; hernias were not uncommon. To avoid a portage, the canoemen might take their chances with the rapids—sometimes with disastrous results. According to research done by the Minnesota Historical Society, fur-trade diaries and journals make mention of more than 60 canoeing accidents. At one spot in a stretch of Basswood River rapids, archaeologists have found a variety of objects from a capsized canoe, including trade axes, spears, beads, hundreds of lead musket balls, and a pewter pipe with tobacco still in the bowl.

The traditional voyageur route through this region became the international border after the Treaty of Paris in 1783. But to the dismay of British fur merchants the boundary gave the United States control of the Grand Portage, the easiest access from Lake Superior to the water routes heading northwest. Despite countless British protests, the boundary remained in place; disputes continued until well into the 20th century. At the tip of Minnesota's northeastern "arrowhead," Grand Portage National Monument preserves mementos of days when the voyageurs labored on the carries and paddled 16 hours a day.

My companions and I made no attempt to match the voyageur pace. Instead, we dawdled. On hot, sunny afternoons we stretched out on granite ledges, cool and lichen-streaked, or swam in lakes that were surprisingly warm. In the mornings and evenings we fished. Lakes in the BWCAW hold the Minnesota record for the size of northern pike—45 pounds, 12 ounces—and walleye—17 pounds, 8 ounces. Guides Stu and Randy threw back every pike they caught, calling them "hawgs." Too bony, they said, though an Ojibwa Indian later told me that pike, properly prepared, is delicious. Using leeches for bait, we spent hours trying to hook walleye, also known as yellow pikeperch and walleyed pike. In Canada they're called pickerel. Apparently the lunkers were as drowsy as we were. We caught only six fish, none large, but they melted in our mouths as we sat back and watched the northern lights flare in the sky.

With all the fresh air and clear, drinkable water around, pollution for once seemed a distant worry. Yet a relative newcomer to the blacklist of pollutants has

Last permanent resident in the Boundary Waters Canoe Area Wilderness, 76-year-old Dorothy Molter offers refreshment to paddlers at her summer home—a wall tent at Knife Lake. In winter she retires to the warmth and solitude of a cabin nearby.

Between neighboring paper mills the Rainy River weaves a twisting boundary, edging the cities of International Falls in Minnesota (at left) and Fort Frances in Ontario. Deep-freeze winters here make news in the U.S. with dispatches from International Falls, self-styled Ice Box of the Nation. Temperatures can dip to 40° below zero F.

begun to cause worry here: acid rain, which is rain or snow that contains significant amounts of sulfuric and nitric acid. Oxides of sulfur and nitrogen, released by smelters, internal-combustion engines, and coal-burning power plants, chemically react with water vapor to form the acids.

Acid rain became an environmental specter in North America in the 1970s, when scientists began finding "dead lakes" in eastern Canada and the northeastern United States. High amounts of acid in the water were killing aquatic life, including whole populations of fish. Evidence pointed to possible harm to forests and human health.

The issue has thrown a shadow on relations between the two countries. According to scientific estimates, some 50 percent of the acid rain falling on Canada can be traced to wind-borne particles from the United States—particularly from the tall stacks in the industrial belt of the upper Ohio River Valley. From 10 to 15 percent of the acid rain in the northeastern United States is said to originate in Canada. Fearing for the health of its two largest industries—forest products and tourism—the Canadian government has pledged itself to reduce sulfur emissions by half in the next decade. And it has demanded that its neighbor also take tougher steps to halt pollution at the source. The U.S. government, while acknowledging the seriousness of the problem, insisted that links between industrial emissions and acid rain were not yet conclusive enough to justify cleanup programs that could cost billions. The government was willing to increase funds for research, but environmentalists and some members of Congress sought stronger action. "Have all the lakes and trees to die before we do something about it?" complained Alex Manson, a Canadian environmental official whom I met in Ottawa. "At this point neither one of our countries can clean up its own problems. Both of us have to do something."

Anxieties about acid rain have surfaced in Quetico and the BWCAW with the near-completion of a coal-burning power plant at Atikokan, 50 miles north of the border. More than half of the thousands of lakes in the area are vulnerable; rocks and soil near them lack enough natural alkalinity, such as that found in limestone, to neutralize acid runoff. Officials in Ontario claim the plant will burn low-sulfur coal and therefore will comply with environmental guidelines.

Meanwhile, on an overgrown hilltop 20 miles east of Ely technicians collect air and water samples for a joint U.S.-Canadian monitoring station. Though acidity varies greatly with individual rainstorms, damage to trees and waters from acid rain has not yet been demonstrated here. But environmentalists plead for action to reduce acidity *before* the damage appears in this unspoiled lakeland.

About 175 miles northwest of the canoeing wilderness a chip of the United States seems to float above the border. This tiny peninsula jutting from Manitoba into Lake of the Woods is part of Minnesota. One might suppose that U.S. boundary negotiators knew secretly that this odd, displaced fragment was rich in sawtimber or rare minerals. How else explain its inclusion in the U.S.?

Actually the Northwest Angle, as it is called, is 130 square miles of swampy forest. The border quirk came about simply because of geographic ignorance combined with American stubbornness. Boundary specifications in the Treaty of Paris ran the line to the extreme northwest point of Lake of the Woods, then due west to the Mississippi River. But such a line would never find the Mississippi. The river rises more than a hundred miles *south* of the lake.

Decades before Lake Itasca was found to be the source of the Mississippi, the British became aware that the treaty line would not achieve their goal: access to navigation on the great river. They asked for a new line that would meet the Mississippi. It would also give them most of northern Minnesota. The Americans refused. Soon the Louisiana Purchase added another complication by extending the U.S. boundaries far beyond the Mississippi. What would be the northern limit of this vast territory?

By an agreement in 1818 the northern boundary ran south from the northwestern corner of Lake of the Woods to join the 49th parallel, which it followed westward to the "Stony Mountains." On the United States side of that line lay the cartographic blip known as the Northwest Angle.

Today the Angle—the northernmost point of the contiguous United States—is primarily a state forest and Indian reservation, though no Indians live here. The one settlement, Angle Inlet, with a year-round population of 50, consists of a bar, a log post office, a one-room schoolhouse, some fishing resorts, and a scattering of cottages. A few year-rounders live on nearby islands.

Once a celebrated sticking point between the U.S. and Canada, the Northwest Angle has now receded into placid obscurity. At the Pine Creek Bar one day sat Kirk Peterson, a native who left home to serve in the Marines and had recently returned to do some guiding and carpentry work. In his 20s, with long blond hair, Kirk stared into his beer and smiled at the thought of his hometown. He had remembered something else unique about it. "I don't think," he mused, "that I've met anyone anywhere who has ever heard of this place."

Necessities for locals and sportsmen alike line the shelves of the Oak Island general store in Lake of the Woods. Storekeeper Ronald Webb (in shirt sleeves) also serves as U.S. customs-immigration officer and fire warden; his wife, Grace (center), doubles as postmaster. Pilot Garland Bernhardt, who operates a charter and guide service, displays a string of walleye, Minnesota's state fish and the most popular species in the border area. To the west of the island—one of 14,600 in the lake—a southward turn of the boundary sets off the lonely bit of land known as the Northwest Angle, northernmost point of the conterminous United States. On the Ontario shore, where Kenora stands today, the railroad shantytown of Rat Portage sprang up in the late 1800s—wallowing in whiskey and wickedness, "the roughest town in Canada" in its day, notes one historian.

FOLLOWING PAGES: Southern leg of the Trans-Canada Highway leads travelers west along the edge of Quetico Provincial Park and the historic waterways of the fur trade. Sunset rays, reflected in the power lines, add a touch of carnival midway.

A Chance
for Paradise

From Sundown, Manitoba, to Sweetgrass, Montana

T he oldest house I saw in the southeast corner of Manitoba had "1902" carved into a thick ceiling beam. Signs announcing a historical site led me to a country church erected in 1899. The area's oldest and only hotel was built in 1926. The blocky white frame building sat like an anvil on the main street of Tolstoi, named for the Russian novelist.

From the look of things history was a mere sapling in these parts. Whereas towns on the New Brunswick-Maine border were celebrating their 200th birthdays, and cities on the Great Lakes were refurbishing 19th-century neighborhoods, here on the plains some of the founders of settlements had only recently died. Watching a modern mower cutting alfalfa, it is not difficult to imagine a lone figure with a scythe doing the same work not very long ago.

Yet there's something about this region east of the Red River of the North that contradicts such a slender historic memory. It's the musty air of the Old World. Sniff it and the area ages, suddenly becoming more rooted in time than many of the older places to the east.

I caught the first breath of a far-reaching past south of Sundown, Manitoba, less than a mile from the border. On this Sunday morning in August the sun glinted off the dome and filtered through the stained-glass windows of the Ukrainian Orthodox Church of St. Elias. The filtered light, abetted by candleglow, reached up to golden stars painted on the sky-blue vault. As worshipers arrived for High Mass, they walked to the front and kissed an icon that had found its way here from Odessa, the old Ukrainian port on the Black Sea.

Men sat on the right, women on the left. Occasionally a priest swung a censer, and little palm-scented clouds drifted upward, signifying the prayers rising to heaven. Led by a cantor, the congregation answered the invocations with singing that sounded like medieval chant. In the constant joining of voices and in the kissing of icons before, during, and after the service I sensed an intense devotion. A tradition of worship tied together places and centuries stretched far apart. Time did stand still in this tiny country church. Well, almost. The priest apologized for the absence of young people at the service. They were playing in a softball tournament in Sundown. *(Continued on page 112)*

Testament to the Old World's enduring presence, domed cupolas and triple-barred crosses crown the Ukrainian Orthodox church in Vita, Manitoba. Free land and freedom of religion drew tens of thousands from Eastern Europe to Canada's prairies.

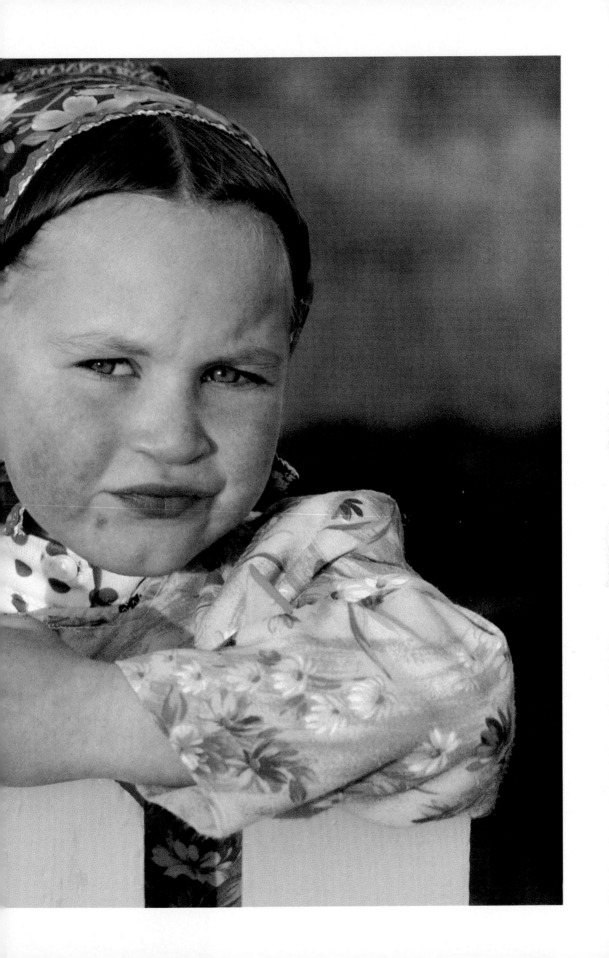

Erecting their own paradise on earth, members of Hillside Colony—a 9,000-acre Hutterite community near Sweetgrass, Montana—roof a new barn. All males wear black, with lads like Peter Wurtz (far left) and brother Tim (left) sporting homemade caps rather than hats. Unlike the Amish, whom they superficially resemble, Hutterites embrace electricity, tractors, and other products of modern technology. They speak German and live communally, sharing all property, taking meals in a central dining hall, trusting to the simple dictates of their 16th-century creed: pacifism, thrift, and industry.

PRECEDING PAGES: Secure behind Hillside Colony's kindergarten fence, five-year-old Laura Wurtz looks askance at the world beyond. In her ordered world little girls may wear bright floral prints, but the young obey the old and women defer to men.

111

Along much of the border on the Manitoba side I was constantly discovering remnants of cultures that harked back to the Old World. Besides the Ukrainians, I met groups of Mennonites and Hutterites, their roots dating from the 1500s in German-speaking Anabaptist communities. Religious persecution spread them far and wide, forcing them into protective, self-sufficient bands. And so they remain, retaining the German language and upholding tradition.

The flood of immigrants began in the late 1800s, when prospective settlers found eager benefactors on both sides of the border. In 1869 Canada purchased from the Hudson's Bay Company the immense tract known as Rupert's Land and North Western Territory—2.5 million square miles of western and northern Canada, more than half the area of the modern nation. Canada was anxious to populate this wilderness. Pamphlets touting the new province of Manitoba as "the garden of the Northwest" were distributed overseas. Even farmers from the States were urged to move north. In the lively competition for settlers, Minnesota and Iowa circulated horror stories of hapless Dakota farmers plagued by drought, blizzards, grasshoppers, and Indian scalp hunters. But the prairies of the Red River Valley, as a North Dakota historian has written, "lay ready and waiting, without stone, stump, or tree to hinder the plow." One settler in Dakota Territory composed a glowing come-on in rhyme: "Though Adam took his wife's advice/And got expelled from Paradise/You'll find another just as nice. . . ." And when talk arose of fertile homestead land running short, Canada advertised its open spaces as the "Last Best West."

To the newcomers the promise of a paradise on earth was more than a rhymester's fancy. Where else could one find so much free land or freedom of religion? To pacifists such as the Mennonites and Hutterites, Canada also offered exemption from military service.

The first large group of Ukrainians arrived in Winnipeg, Manitoba, in 1896. With most of the desirable homestead land taken, they were directed to a marginal area near the border. Not even the sight of sandy, rock-studded bottomland could dismay the pioneers, according to Luba Onysko, the daughter of an immigrant of the early 1900s. I met her in the small, somnolent town of Gardenton, where she lives in the house with the Canadian flag outside. Luba operates the post office from her home. "In the old country," she explained, "they were so short of stone and brush to build things and heat their homes that when they saw all the stones and brush here they thought they were in heaven."

At Stuartburn, Mary Matichuk told me of her grandfather who "actually dug a hole in the ground and that's where he spent his first winter." The settlers eventually raised log homes and broke the tough prairie sod for their farms. Often cash ran short. Some pioneers worked the winters in Minnesota lumber camps. For others buffalo provided a first cash crop—long after the great herds had been wiped out. Bleached buffalo bones bestrewed the prairies; pioneers shipped them east to sugar refiners. Bone char removes the color from sugar.

In Manitoba immigrants laid track for the Canadian Pacific Railway, the nation's first transcontinental railroad. By 1910 some 75,000 Ukrainians had come to the province, an influx that disturbed many of English stock. Immigration minister Clifford Sifton met the criticism head-on: "I think a stalwart peasant in a sheepskin coat, born on the soil, whose forefathers have been farmers

Coursing the continental heartland from Lake of the Woods to the Rockies, the border skirts prairie farms and ranches—a broad sprawl of open sky, small towns, and elemental beauty. Britain and the U.S. had sought natural borders based on watersheds, then in 1818 agreed on the 49th parallel—and yielded the land on either side of it.

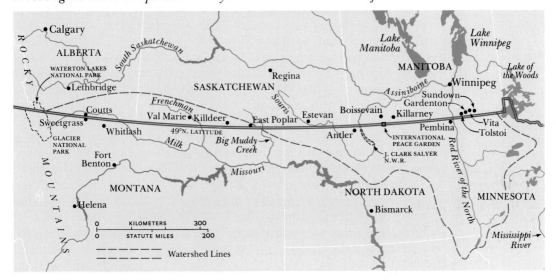

for ten generations, with a stout wife and a half-dozen children, is good quality." Many of the Ukrainian Canadians I met along the border still wear their past on their sleeves. Schools teach the Ukrainian language as well as native dances and crafts. In the town of Vita a restaurant offered borscht, cabbage rolls, and savory turnovers called pirogi. Southeast Manitoba contains 35 Ukrainian churches, most with the distinctive dome.

From this corner of the province I headed west, due west, on a country road that ran straight and true. No curves, no hills, no loops. Just the intoxicating horizon. After more than a thousand miles of a landscape hemmed by forest, the endless vista on the open plains made me want to drive and drive into the distance. I wouldn't have to stop, I mused, until I met the formidable wall of the Rocky Mountains.

The plains looked archetypal: flat, stretched out, rippling with row crops or lying dark and fallow; farmhouses and barns tucked behind the windbreak of a few trees; brightly painted grain elevators standing like sentinels along the railroad tracks. Overhead spread a great arch of sky. smudged here and there with rain showers slanting across the land.

Harvest was in full swing. Combines plodded back and forth, trailing clouds of dust. Bales of alfalfa were stacked in varied shapes—pyramids, mausoleums, loaves of bread. Farther west the fields turned more to wheat and barley; at dusk their golden stubble shone like sandy beaches. As night fell the red running lights of combines pricked the darkness. The land was yielding its fruit.

West of the Red River I came upon tiny farming communities with German names—Schanzenfeld, Blumenort, Hochfeld, Gnadenthal, Osterwick. These were villages of Mennonites, clinging to an evangelical faith opposed to holding office, taking loyalty oaths, and other signs of allegiance to worldly rule. Thousands of Mennonite settlers had arrived in Manitoba from Russia in the 1870s; many homesteaded near the border where farming conditions reminded them of the dry steppes they had cultivated in the Old World.

They came just after the province was established, a step taken in part to keep the vast hinterland a part of Canada. Steamboats had arrived, and a busy north-south traffic had developed along the Red River Valley between Winnipeg and the Mississippi River port of St. Paul, Minnesota. Boosters of the booming port, coveting Canada's prairies as "the lawful and natural prey of the American eagle," recruited allies among the Canadian métis, the proud buffalo hunters of mixed Indian and European lineage.

I paused at Pembina, North Dakota, where the Red River crosses the border; here a small museum preserves the memory of an old fort and of the métis hunting rendezvous in the mid-19th century. To the métis the border was invisible. Entire families arrived in the famed Red River carts, the squealing of ungreased wheels heralding their approach for miles ahead. At Pembina the hunters elected a governor, captains, and guides. Each morning a priest offered Mass and drilled the children in catechism. The nights were merry with song and dance. With the coming of Canadian government and a wave of settlers, the métis resisted encroachment on prairie lands. Louis Riel, an extraordinary leader educated in law and religion, a mystic and at times a madman, led métis risings in 1869 and 1885. In the latter year he was tried and hanged.

And so the settlers continued to flow in, seeking their new paradise. As I roamed the farmlands beside the 49th parallel I thought that Canada could hardly have done better than to populate its border with pious folk whose religion and community strength depended on their stewardship of the land. Once these immigrants settled, threats to the border dissolved.

The Hutterites' Mayfair Colony, ten miles southeast of Killarney, Manitoba, presented an impressive sight from the road. Its skyline of grain elevators and storage bins gave it the look of a well-heeled corporate farm. Yet driving to its center I saw bearded men dressed in dark clothes and suspenders, women in long dresses and aprons, with scarves on their heads—people who seemed to have stepped out of the 16th century. "Christian communism" is how one writer described Hutterite collectives, in which several families share property and profits. Like the Mennonites, the Hutterites joined the land rush to the New World in the 1870s. In the U.S. their refusal to bear arms during the Spanish-American War and World War I caused considerable resentment, however. Finally they felt compelled to move to Canada. Today more than 200 colonies are established in western Canada. Over the years Hutterite groups have also returned to the United States, settling mainly in the Dakotas and Montana.

At Mayfair the colony's president, looking patriarchal in full gray beard, was at first reluctant to allow me to walk about and interview the residents. Jacob Gross maintained that the 63 members of the colony must remain as aloof as possible from activities that could distract them from work and from devotion to God. The colony even had a rule barring TV and radio; picture taking was frowned upon, and visits to town other than for business were discouraged.

Yet Hutterites are extremely proud of their accomplishments. At Mayfair

Not one to sit back and watch when his hometown began to die, retired rancher Harley "Bud" Kissner of Antler, North Dakota, offered free parcels of land to young families. His giveaway, widely publicized, drew a flood of applicants; those selected brought enough children to reopen the Antler school. Its closing in 1981 had prodded Kissner into action.

they have a thriving 5,000-acre farm that is largely self-sufficient. "Oh, let him see the place," one of the other elders finally said. "We've never had anyone write about our colony." The president relented. His brother Ernest, the colony's beekeeper, escorted me.

One can easily be misled by the rustic appearance and hermetic society here. Unlike the Amish, whose communities also grew out of the 16th-century Anabaptist movement but who still use horses to plow their fields, the Hutterites embrace modern technology. The metalworking shop, the blacksmith's shop, the cobbler's shop—everything appeared to be new and immaculate. In a spacious metal barn 3,000 hogs squealed and snorted as we walked by. When I recoiled at the pungent odor, Ernest smiled: "It smells like money, that's what they say." He pointed out innovative features, some devised by the Hutterites themselves: a conveyor belt that removes the manure, a sophisticated system for air circulation and heat exchange, and self-feeders for the young pigs.

The Hutterites have become a major force in agribusiness. In Manitoba the colonies produce nearly two-thirds of the market hogs and nine-tenths of the market geese. And how you keep the youngsters down on the farm is not a worrisome question. Once a Hutterite child reaches 15, he leaves the colony school for full-time work on the farm. Few children defect to the world outside.

When I remarked on how prosperous the Mayfair farm appeared, the reply was, "If you don't work, you have nothing to *(Continued on page 123)*

FOLLOWING PAGES: Blizzard of snow geese descends on J. Clark Salyer National Wildlife Refuge near Antler. Prime habitat, including Souris River marshes, makes Salyer an important stopover and nesting area for migratory birds on the Central flyway.

Hoodoos and hideaways haunt a stretch of Montana badlands near Sweetgrass, where erosion carves soft sandstone and harder cap rock into weird shapes. Known locally as Jerusalem Rocks—the name apparently stems from a shepherd who called the area Little Jerusalem—these formations overlook Hutterite grainfields (opposite) blanketing a broad channel gouged 10,000 years ago by glacial melt.

*P*atterns of the fall: Stubble fires race across grainfields, while in another tract golden stripes of harvested fields alternate with bands of fallow (opposite). Such multihued landscapes reflect lessons of Dust Bowl days. With ribbons of planted land, farmers seek to curb wind erosion on their fallow acres. American farmers use controlled burning against pests and unwanted vegetation, and to make tilling easier; but Canadian authorities discourage it as wasteful of moisture and organic matter. Pioneer farmers dreaded prairie wildfire, fire that overleaped rivers and flew faster than a horse could run. "Even cow chips," writes Stephen J. Pyne in *Fire in America*, "sailing like flaming frisbees before high winds . . . were a major threat to isolated farms and towns."

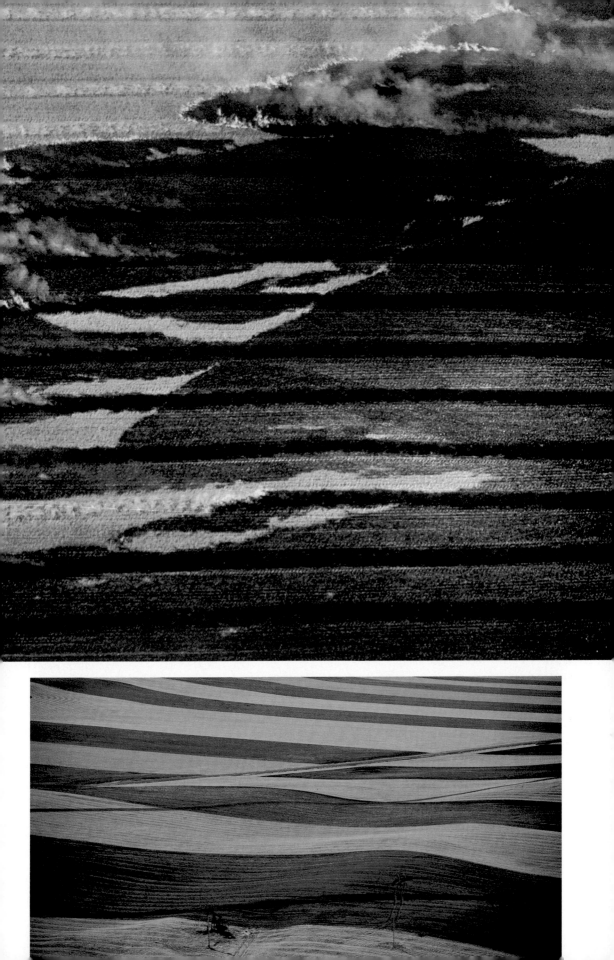

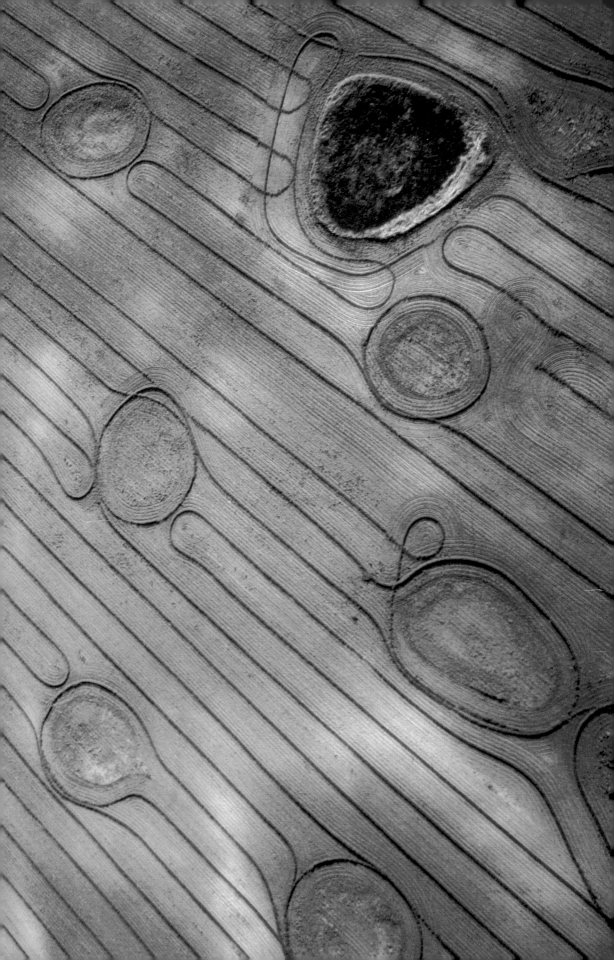

show, that's how we figure it." As I prepared to leave, Ernest's wife, Eda, suddenly began to worry about me. Ignoring my protests, she gave me five sandwiches—"so you don't have to buy any"—and a watermelon with a spoon and knife—"so you don't have to buy any drinks." Well provisioned and with Ernest having wiped the dust off the outside mirror of my car, I left the Hutterites and their fascinating version of the promised land.

Not far from the border in Antler, North Dakota—population around a hundred and dwindling—the practice of homesteading has been dusted off for the 1980s. The idea was the brainstorm of Rick Jorgensen, a young go-getter who likes antiques—apparently including small towns—and Harley "Bud" Kissner, a rancher in his 70s. Kissner remembers with nostalgia the time, 60 years ago, when Antler buzzed with crowds and commerce. In 1981, when Antler's only remaining school closed, Jorgensen and Kissner feared the last school bell would sound the death knell for the town. Antler needed newcomers, the two men concluded, newcomers with a lot of school-age children.

So Kissner decided to give away land. The recipients would have to stay for five years—as in the 19th-century homesteading days—and enroll their children in the Antler elementary school. Kissner, semiretired, felt he could spare the property from his 640-acre farm. Jorgensen drew up a newspaper ad with the headline FREE LAND, and a wire service spread the story across the country. Antler became an overnight sensation.

In a single day 3,000 phone calls came into the town, disrupting local service. Letters poured in; people from as far away as Germany and Australia wanted to live in Antler. At his home outside of town Bud, a bachelor, showed me some of the boxes filled with letters. They were amazing documents, full of cries for help and salvation. A typical one began, "We were sitting in our living room wondering where our life was going when out of frustration I switched on the news, and there you were with the answer to our dreams."

Six families received plots of nine or five acres. In the fall of 1981 the school reopened, and two years later two-thirds of the 27 children enrolled belonged to "homesteader" families. Yet the dreams envisioned in those boxes of letters still seem distant. The families live in trailers or in houses moved from other sites to a road east of Kissner's house—homesteads huddled together on the windy, open plain. The newcomers have struggled to make ends meet.

Hope and determination, the staples of homesteaders past, persist in Antler today. The Ellis family in its first year was at times reduced to little more than biscuits for dinner. But Barbara Ellis, mother of eight, stressed that her family had few regrets about uprooting in Utah and coming to Antler. Though still in debt, the Ellises have bought a cow and have harvested the first corn, beans, and tomatoes from their garden. Mike, the father, has begun a successful welding business. "I look at our future here as something sure," Barbara said. "But it is not something we will get all at once. It will come slowly."

From Lake of the Woods to the Rockies the border through this prairie

Unintentional art scrolls a fallow field near the North Dakota-Manitoba border, where summer-sown flax strips, coiling around the prairie potholes, help anchor the soil— a sod-bound abstraction that mirrors the work of Miró.

heartland follows the 49th parallel for 860 miles. In the boundary negotiations this was probably the least contentious of all the sections. Agreement was reached in 1818, but no official survey was made until the 1870s, when both countries were promoting settlement. The survey was long overdue; by then the boundary at the Red River crossing had been marked at five different places. As the British and American surveying teams made their way west, they must have resembled invading forces; each commission numbered about 270 people, counting teamsters, herders, couriers, and military escorts. They used a variety of boundary markers, including huge mounds of sod. These were replaced in the early 1900s by four-foot-high cast-iron monuments that can still be seen along the remote border roads.

Apprehensive of Indian attacks, the U.S. sent part of the Seventh Cavalry to accompany the boundary commission in 1873. Three years later more than 250 men of the Seventh were annihilated by the Sioux and Cheyenne in the Battle of the Little Bighorn. After the battle Sitting Bull and his Sioux followers took refuge in Canada. The great chief viewed the border as a convenient remedy, referring to it as the Medicine Line.

The slaughter at the Little Bighorn shocked a nation celebrating its 100th birthday. How much more ominous the weapons of war on the northern plains a century later. East of Antler I came upon a nuclear missile site. Some 300 Minuteman III missiles, each with three warheads, have been buried in underground silos within a corridor south of the border—part of the nation's defenses in the nuclear age. I stood before a chain link fence enclosing what looked to be an enormous trapdoor painted in camouflage. Underneath, I presumed, nestled a missile with the explosive force of 335,000 tons of TNT. A sign on the fence read: No Trespassing. Use of Deadly Force Authorized.

Not far away I came upon a more comforting symbol of international relations. On the border between Dunseith, North Dakota, and Boissevain, Manitoba, near the midpoint of the continent, Canada and the United States have established a 2,339-acre International Peace Garden.

A hundred and fifty miles to the west the town of Estevan, Saskatchewan, with a population of 10,000, is a virtual metropolis along the grasslands border. The lignite—soft coal—strip-mined around Estevan fuels a power plant on a tributary of the nearby Souris River, supplying much of the province's electricity. Estevan also serves as a center for oil and gas fields to the north and east.

For a mining town full of men making good wages, Estevan appeared surprisingly tranquil; it had none of the hard-nailed, transient qualities of many mining towns in the U.S. No doubt Canada has its tough ones also, but the contrast in Estevan seemed remarkable. When I mentioned this, Canadians pointed to differences in the ways the two countries settled their western frontiers.

South of the border, homesteaders and fortune seekers often devised their own rules of conduct, having arrived in advance of any meaningful government authority. The western frontier won a reputation for lawlessness, with outlaw gangs, vigilantes, and range wars. Canada's frontier bore a different image, one based on strong visible government. The government might have had its hands full in such rip-roaring railroad towns as Rat Portage, Ontario; yet the image remains valid. "We had no wild west," writes Canadian historian Pierre Berton.

The Mounties achieved notable success against the cross-border whiskey traffic in Whoop-Up days.Much more so than the latter-day enforcers who tried to stanch the southward flow during Prohibition in the United States, from 1919 to 1933.It is a rare town on the border that has no tales of rum-running in its past.I often heard eyewitness accounts of big black sedans filled with liquor racing down back roads at night, or transactions in "boozoriums" and "blind pigs"—the liquor depots and speakeasies that catered to the vast American thirst.Liquor could move legally in Canada, and suppliers prospered. Out of that Prohibition traffic grew world-class fortunes.

As I continued my westward journey past mile after mile of grainfields, it struck me that the most effective tamer of the west was not the police, or the railroad, or the immigrants, but the plow. The sod-breaking plow had transformed a wilderness of grass into a seemingly endless grid of rich croplands dotted with no-frills farm towns.The change from prairie to farmland was described in elegiac fashion by Canadian writer Mary Hiemstra in her autobiography, *Gully Farm*:

"The wind is still sweet, but there is no wildness in it and it no longer seems to have wandered a great way over grass and trees and flowers.It now smells of dry straw and bread."

There are places where the scent of wildflowers and the rustle of tall grasses can still arrest the senses, however. From the approximate point where the Montana-North Dakota border touches Saskatchewan to where the Milk River flows from Montana into Alberta—a span of some 400 miles—extensive pockets of unplowed grassland remain.The terrain is too rugged for planting, as in the valleys of the Frenchman River and Big Muddy Creek, or too arid and remote, as in the vicinity of the Milk River.Cattle grazing becomes the chief form of land use, and a diverse natural community persists. Deep, tree-lined coulees shelter white-tailed and mule deer. Golden eagles nest on tawny buttes.Spear grass, once the diet of bison, blankets the valley floors, and on the ridges cactus flares with bright, opulent flowers.At night coyotes yip and holler in their eerie serenades. Shrinkage of the prairie acreage, however, has imperiled such denizens as the black-footed ferret and the swift fox.

(Continued on page 134)

*L*ike the awesome bison herds that roamed here, the original grasslands endure only in fragments. To preserve species of the mixed-grass prairie (below opposite), Canada's proposed Grasslands National Park would set aside some 350 square miles in southern Saskatchewan. Here Canada also protects its last remaining colonies of black-tailed prairie dogs: "Dogtown Road" (right) leads to one of the rodent towns. At a bluff called the Snake Pit, a prairie rattler flicks a forked tongue, sensing the air at an intruder's approach.

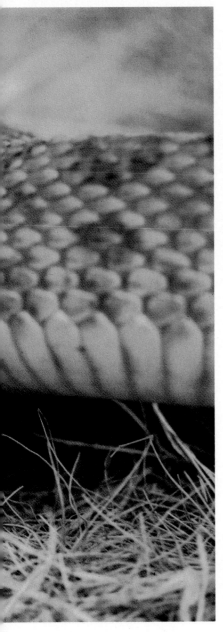

"Quiet earth, big sky." So Wallace Stegner, novelist and conservationist, wrote of his childhood home in southern Saskatchewan. There stark, treeless flatlands foster a sense of expansive emptiness, and "human intrusions seem as abrupt as the elevators that leap out of the plain to announce every little hamlet." These two elevators, owned by the Pioneer Grain Company, punctuate the plain near the community of East Poplar, some five miles north of the border.

*A*t home on the range, cowboys return to a ranch near Montana's Sweet Grass Hills after taking bulls to winter pasture. Though cattle predominate, some ranchers here raise bison as well; they need less care and survive dry times better. The area takes its name from a native grass, Hierochloe odorata; its vanilla-like smell lent a sweet fragrance to Indian ritual. Today most of the sweet grass has gone the way of the bison.

PRECEDING PAGES: Moonrise over the Sweet Grass Hills recalls the words of the 19th-century adventurer, Capt. William Francis Butler: "No solitude can equal the loneliness of a night-shadowed prairie: one feels the stillness, and hears the silence, the wail of the prowling wolf makes the voice of solitude audible, the stars look down through infinite silence upon a silence almost as intense."

Contrasting land uses define the border in this Landsat image, taken some 560 miles above the earth. The slanting line distinguishes Alberta rangeland, in dark hues (the darkest suggesting overgrazing), from Montana wheatland, shown in shades of tan. The reddish patch at lower left marks the well-vegetated Sweet Grass Hills.

GEOPIC TM/EARTH SATELLITE CORPORATION

In view of the significance of the prairie as a part of the nation's heritage, Canada has targeted up to 350 square miles for a grasslands national park. The land lies between Val Marie and Killdeer in southwestern Saskatchewan and includes the scenic Killdeer badlands. Among the area's major attractions are Canada's last existing colonies of black-tailed prairie dogs.

Delays in acquisition of land have stirred concern for the park proposal. But Parks Canada revived hopes with the announcement that it had acquired 3,106 acres, a major component of the park's western sector.

I ventured into the grasslands with Fernand Perrault, a rancher, and his wife, Lise, a painter of prairie scenes. The Perraults wanted to catch a few rattlesnakes for the small museum they operate in their Val Marie home. We rode the bumpy ridgelines to an eroding sandstone bluff dubbed the Snake Pit. Each year scores of prairie rattlesnakes have their young here and then hibernate for the winter in cracks along the slopes. The Perraults began to poke cautiously into the crevices, Fernand using a converted hockey stick with a clamp on the end, and Lise wielding a mop handle. In an hour they had captured three snakes. Usually we heard the discomfiting rattle before we saw the snake, so well did the tan-and-brown skin pattern blend with the ground. Under one rock we saw a Medusa's head of writhing newborn snakes, thin as pencils.

All the talk about preserving the prairie and its life forms had apparently had some effect on Fernand. As he dropped a wriggling, tongue-flicking snake into a can, he mused, "You know, I grew up where I was taught to shoot every rattler I saw. I'm still tempted to, but I also just like to watch them now."

On my summer drive along the sparsely populated grasslands border I was struck by the isolation of many of the customs stations. They stood literally in the middle of nowhere, on quiet country roads, surrounded by empty space. Some recorded only four or five vehicles a day. Many are open only during normal working hours; to reach the nearest 24-hour station often requires a detour of an hour or more.

The busiest crossing on the plains is at Sweetgrass, Montana, and Coutts, Alberta. It is on the main highway along the eastern side of the Rockies, a route to Alaska. On an average day about 500 vehicles pass through customs here. By contrast, the Peace Bridge between Buffalo, New York, and Fort Erie, Ontario, the single most heavily traveled crossing, averages 9,000 a day.

A border agent's job at Sweetgrass and Coutts does not end with checking ID and destination. Here the agent must be prepared to verify the contents of a freight train, monitor a pipeline carrying natural gas from Canada into the United States, decipher a veterinarian's report on livestock in transit, and examine private aircraft that use the grass landing strip on the border swath. The staff at Sweetgrass, I was told, enforces the laws of 81 different agencies.

The emphasis on the U.S. side tends toward criminal law enforcement. Agents wear revolvers; they search vehicles for drugs more frequently than on the Canadian side and use computers to check whether a driver is wanted by the law or has a criminal record that could bar him from the country. The Canadians stress revenue collecting. Their agents go unarmed, and the computers are used exclusively to control the movement of goods and process other information relating to the sizable commercial truck traffic here.

From the very start of my journey I asked customs agents why they would search one person's vehicle and not another's. Invariably they told me that they were provided with behavioral profiles of possible lawbreaking types. They also relied on a "sixth sense" to alert them to suspicious traits. Since I hated being searched or closely questioned, I tried to figure out an avoidance strategy. I tried leaving maps open on the seat, or I yawned right before I pulled up to the customs window, or I listened to Rachmaninoff instead of the Rolling Stones. None of these stratagems meant anything, I was sorry to learn, when I spent a few hours with the night crew at Coutts. The supervisor suddenly called out, "Let's blitz 'em!" For the next 45 minutes his agents searched every car that came through—18 of them— whether the drivers yawned or not.

I was less than a hundred miles from the Rocky Mountains and the end of the Great Plains when in early September I finally got an inside look at a harvest. Back in August on the Manitoba-North Dakota line, the harvest had been going at full tilt, with no time for a visitor's interruptions. In eastern Montana drought had all but ruled out any extensive grain cutting. But at 4,000 feet in the upland plains near Montana's Sweet Grass Hills, the barley was just ripening.

"The field looks tick," exclaimed Dennis Iverson on a bright cool morning, borrowing a phrase of his grandfather's to indicate that the crop looked healthy and dry and ready to come down. With that he sent three combines rumbling out on a golden, 90-acre field. Dennis, the fourth generation of Iversons to farm in north-central Montana, owns 7,000 acres north of the crossroads town of Whitlash, his land within eyeshot of Canada. On 2,000 acres he grows wheat and barley. On the remainder of his property he runs a small herd of cattle and manages a number of oil wells owned by his father. In addition Dennis represents District 12 in Montana's House of Representatives and actively promotes cooperation between lawmakers on both sides of the border, while his wife, Donna, promotes the cause of education in the region.

The ungainly combines set off three abreast, their 24-foot-wide cutting heads mowing down the tightly spaced rows of barley. For the harvest Dennis had hired a team of custom cutters; he finds it cheaper to pay the team each year than to buy combines at $100,000 apiece and worry about the myriad repairs. He figures the cutters cost him $14 an acre.

If all goes according to plan, the harvest will take on an obsessive rhythm, the machines grinding for 18 hours a day, not even stopping as the drivers unload the threshed grain into dump trucks alongside. To keep moving is the imperative of the harvest; winter can never be far behind.

Dennis's 18-year-old son, Mike, passed the hours in the air-conditioned cab of a combine by listening to rock and daydreaming. Don Pollington, leader of the cutting team, preferred the "music of the combines"; his ear was attuned to sounds of trouble in the machinery. Unfortunately, his morning was filled with discordant notes—a lost wheel, a broken belt, a tangle of slightly damp barley.

Home-cooked food and plenty of it—compliments of Donna Iverson—fuels the hired harvesters on the Iverson barley fields near Whitlash, Montana. Bringing meals to the workers keeps them on the job longer. With the crop ready and the weather right the crews put in 16-to-18-hour days—the age-old regimen of making hay while the sun shines.

Within three hours not a single combine was working. Don was still able to strike a cheery note: "Well, it could be snowing."

Overnight a storm from the northwest drenched the fields, leaving them too wet to cut. No one was visibly upset, though. A farmer puts in long hours learning to become a stoic. That same year a freak July hailstorm had ruined a hundred acres of winter wheat, turning a good year into a break-even one. "There was no point in getting excited," Dennis said. "Yet it gripes me a little. Drought is one thing; you can see it coming. Hailstorms do seem unfair."

Clouds the color of eggplants hung low in the sky for the next several days of my visit, bringing scattered rain. Waiting for the fields to dry, the cutting crew tinkered with the combines or engaged in rough-and-tumble basketball games in the workshed. One night a group of us attended a harvest dance.

Eventually Dennis left for a legislative conference in Alaska, and soon afterward his son Mike departed to start school. The cutters dispersed as well, saying they would return as soon as the fields dried. Still, no one seemed worried. The sun would come out, the fields would be cut, the grain would go to market. Those of little faith do not last on the plains.

FOLLOWING PAGES: Sweet Grass Hills bask in the sunshine while a trio of combines cuts a 72-foot swath through the Iverson fields. The harvesting crews move from farm to farm, north with the ripening crops, until the bounty of the heartland has been harvested.

To Touch
the Sky

To climb to the top of Mount Cleveland, the tallest peak in Glacier National Park at 10,466 feet, takes something of the stamina of an elk and the sure-footedness of a mountain goat. At least that's what seven humans came to believe after traveling on elk and goat trails in a scramble to the rooftop of northwestern Montana.

The expedition began in Alberta, in adjoining Waterton Lakes National Park; together the two parks form an international peace park along the Continental Divide. Photographer Mike Yamashita and I, with two guides and three of their mountaineering companions, set off one September dawn in a motor launch southward on Upper Waterton Lake. The air carried a decided nip, harbinger of the cold and snow that grip the parks for as long as eight months a year. As the boat churned through the bumpy water, we kept our eyes fastened on the mist-shrouded peaks ahead. The foreboding look of the dim crags and dark valleys reminded me of a mountain fastness in a fairy tale, with all the intimations of strange creatures and heroic adventures that such tales portend.

We crossed the 49th parallel near the middle of the lake; 14 miles due west rose the highest point on the border south of Alaska—an elevation of 9,500 feet in the Boundary Mountains. This summit was reached by boundary surveyors in 1861; few white men had seen this breathtaking country before then.

The darkness hid the border swath. But though the border may be out of sight, it is never out of mind. Our boatman had an international pilot's license and needed official permission to drop us on the U.S. side. At the end of our seven-mile trip we checked in with a U.S. park ranger who was deputized to serve as a customs official. One of our party, a citizen of Colombia, had her ID ready, but we were waved through and soon had vanished into the woods.

We started off on a clearly defined hiking trail, yet no other footprints greeted us; the off-season had begun. Detouring for a bit, we skirted the marshy Kootenai Lakes—and were rewarded with *(Continued on page 146)*

At summer's end and season's turning fresh snow coats Mount Cleveland, highest peak in Glacier, born in an upheaval of rock layers some 65 million years ago.

FOLLOWING PAGES: Breezing into Canada, cyclists cross the line on the main highway between Glacier and Waterton Lakes parks. Nearby Chief Mountain, a border landmark, reveals evidence of the Lewis Overthrust—the piling of older rock on younger beds.

A bald eagle soars off with a kokanee salmon at Lower McDonald Creek, a choice
fishing spot in Glacier; hundreds of eagles feast on dead and dying salmon here
each fall. Streams and lakes sustain an abundance of wildlife in the twin parks: At Glacier's
Kootenai Lakes a cow moose feeds on aquatic plants; north of the border a mule deer keeps
a heads-up alert as her fawns drink from one of the Waterton lakes.

the sight of a bull moose and his harem of three cows slurping aquatic plants. On the opposite bank a sound like that of a branch cracking made us look up in time to see two leggy young moose jousting with their antlers.

Before long we got the bright idea of taking a shortcut along an elk trail. On a slope crowded with fir and spruce we fought our way through thick underbrush, following a maze of hoof-beaten paths. Often the grade was so steep and the needle-matted ground so loose that most of us embarked on a crashing glissade into more brush below. We also contended with windfalls, some of the downed tree trunks being as big around as wine casks. "Elk just jump right over these trees," Randy Gayner, a guide, said enviously. We on the other hand went up and over with all the grace of dudes clambering onto and off a saddle. Concentrating on our footing, we gave scarcely a thought to the possibility that a grizzly might be dining in one of the berry patches along the route.

On our climb to Cleveland's peak we made base camp at about 5,000 feet along Camp Creek, its swift, cold flow fed by a snowfield that gleamed dully in the evening light. Next morning we woke to strong winds and overcast skies; mountaintops were dusted with fresh snow. Jamming sweaters, jackets, and down vests into day packs, we left camp and began our ascent of the western face of Mount Cleveland, its top lathered in clouds.

As we cleared the tree line the stark panorama of the high Rockies unfolded around us. Everywhere the rough touch of glaciers was in evidence—from the sharp, chiseled ridges, or arêtes, to the steep, hollowed-out bowls called cirques. Waterton-Glacier today holds about 50 glaciers, all of them shrinking.

At 7,000 feet we crossed into a monotonous realm of loose sedimentary rock. On the steep scree slopes we took to switchbacking, gaining only a few feet of altitude with each reversal. Once we picked up a short section of a mountain goat trail that traversed the bare rock face. But even on the trail, without the cloven hoof it was like walking a tightrope. Without a tree, bush, or even a boulder to grab, a slip off the narrow path could send a hiker skidding down the mountainside as part of a rockslide. At one point I dropped to all fours to avoid such a fate. Just short of the ridge crest leading to the summit we came to a halt and, huddling against the razor-sharp wind, wolfed down dried fruit, sausage, and crackers. As we ate, the sun broke through just long enough to transform a drab gray patch of water below us into a brilliant turquoise lake.

At times such as this the actuality of a man-made international border, which lay less than six miles away as the eagle flies, seemed a remote and inconsequential fact of life. At the same time I knew that if any serious accident should befall us, help could be expected from both the Canadian and American sides—a fact *for* life. It is the "everyday working reality," as Glacier Superintendent Robert Haraden puts it, that adds dimension to the symbolism of Waterton-Glacier International Peace Park. Though Waterton Lakes and Glacier are administered separately, a signed agreement calls for mutual aid in emergencies such as fire and search and rescue.

The two parks work especially closely together in bear management. The grizzly, a race of the brown bear, survives in sizable numbers in Alaska and northwestern Canada, but it has disappeared from most of its former range in North America. Grizzlies today number fewer than a thousand below the

Canadian border. Across the million acres of Waterton-Glacier roam 200 to 300 of them—and they are carefully watched. Under a unique monitoring system park observers report each sighting—time, place, and number of bears. The parks use the data to help ensure visitor safety, closing trails, for example, where

"This land of natural splendors is dedicated to peace, one of man's highest goals, and to an international friendship that has few rivals. . . . Like the trails, streams, and valleys of the Rockies, these bonds recognize no boundary." In this spirit the U.S. and Canada united the two parks into Waterton-Glacier International Peace Park. And a joint brochure offers visitors these words in French, Japanese, Spanish, and German as well. Though separately administered, the parks share training and rescue programs—and concern over threats to the environment, which also know no boundary. A planned mining operation in Canada worries Glacier officials: It may pollute southward-flowing waters. The Lewis Overthrust, the phenomenon that raised the breathtaking mountains, also left another legacy: pockets of oil and gas. Animals, following their natural movements, may range beyond park boundaries—and into conflict with neighboring development.

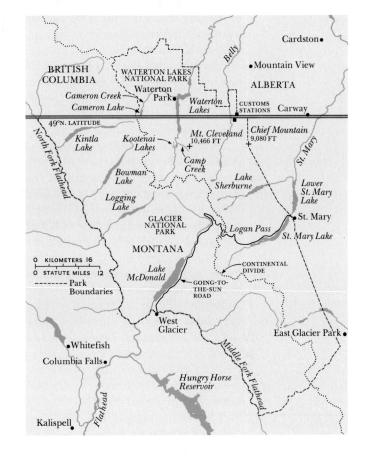

bears are known to be feeding. Oblivious of international borders, the grizzly ranges widely—an average of 190 square miles for adult males.

The bear watch began in 1967, after grizzlies killed two backcountry campers in Glacier. Since then the grizzly has become something of an ominous presence, worrying tourists and park personnel alike. Officials say the surge of visitation to the Glacier backcountry may be causing an increase in confrontations. In 1983 Glacier counted a total of 2.2 million visitors, more than twice the population of Montana. Most visitors never lay eyes on a bear, let alone confront one, but a few encounters result in mauling of humans.

According to current policy, potentially troublesome bears are transported to remote wilds; if they keep returning to visitor areas and repeatedly create a hazard, they may be destroyed. But the parks must also try to avoid needless disruption of the movements and habits of wildlife, notes Glacier resource manager Gary Gregory. "Comments following bear attacks range from 'eliminate all grizzlies from the park' to 'eliminate all people,' " says Gregory. "Obviously the answer is somewhere in the middle."

Backcountry hikers are urged to take special precautions, including making sufficient noise to warn off any grizzlies in the vicinity. The superintendent at Glacier carries an air horn when he hikes; the chief ranger uses a police whistle. During my excursions to the backcountry I never saw a grizzly, though I had a perverse desire to get a good look at one. The most awesome animal I could spot was a brawny bull elk.

In camp that evening we heard elk bugling all around us. The shrill, eerie screams announced that rutting season had begun in earnest. In an attempt to entice an elk into view, Randy Gayner broke off a cow parsnip stem and blew into it. The other guide, David Ames, produced a fiddle and scratched on it with a bow in his effort to mimic the elk. All versions failed.

On the ridge leading to the top of Mount Cleveland I wasn't thinking of grizzlies or elk. I was intent on mustering my strength and reaching the top as quickly as possible. Five hours on the scree slope had nearly exhausted us. Ahead lay the last obstacle—a fractured outcrop of igneous rock. Seeking toeholds, we pulled ourselves up the rock wall and inched along ledges until we stepped out onto the pinnacle of Waterton-Glacier. At two miles high the wind tore at our clothes, and an ice-glazed snowfield stretched away in front of us. Gray-crowned rosy finches dived in and out of crevices, chirping harshly, and a few ravens stood on rocks like grim gargoyles. On a clear day, I had been told, one can count 50 peaks and see as far east as the Sweet Grass Hills in Montana, and as far north as the Matterhorn-like peak of Mount Assiniboine, west of Calgary, both more than a hundred miles away. On this blustery day, though, we were walking through clouds. Visibility was down to a hundred yards, but I still felt like a character in a fairy tale; after all, I could reach up and touch the sky.

Chilled by the driving wind, some of us retreated behind boulders, while the more energetic went on to sign the register on the official summit. Only 19 names had preceded ours that year, we learned. Returning to the group at the brow of the mountain, Cris Coughlin, one of our climbing party, called out:

"Guess what we saw?"

We shook our heads dumbly. "There are grizzly tracks up here!" she cried. Apparently, some bear had climbed up Mount Cleveland to feed on the moths that abound here. We all began to laugh and hoot—not to scare off any high-altitude bear but out of amazed appreciation at the ways of wild creatures. Then, as daylight began to weaken, we shook hands, turned, and hurriedly started our descent. I, for one, was already anticipating that special peace of friends sharing a campsite next to a mountain stream.

Mountain walls funnel stiff winds across the Waterton lakes; the steady buffeting stunts the black cottonwoods growing on a spit of land in Middle Waterton.

FOLLOWING PAGES: Autumn hues herald the season's end for the Prince of Wales Hotel, a chalet-style Waterton resort looking up the valley to the border and the U.S. park beyond. Glaciers carved the valley; retreating, they left the hotel's flat-topped site—part moraine and part kame terrace, the sand and gravel deposited by melt.

*E*njoying the calm before a late-summer storm, Glacier hikers wade through waist-high timothy; next day they would plod through six inches of snow. Such weather keeps most hikers off the trails after September, despite the brilliant foliage. Across the border (right) stately evergreens and 8,268-foot Sofa Mountain rise beyond a fringe of autumn gold.

*H*igh above the cleft of Waterton Valley author O'Neill (at left) and climbing partners Randy Gayner and Cris Coughlin (right) take a rubble slope on all fours. A mile of terrain and several hundred vertical feet separate them from their goal: the summit of Mount Cleveland.

FOLLOWING PAGES: Porcupine Ridge sends glacier-honed quills into the pink borderland sky.

The Other Side
of the Mountains

From the Rockies to Vancouver Island

In the year 1858 the sight of Americans did not exactly inspire feelings of neighborliness north of the border. "The great Yankee unwashed," one observer branded the foreigners, as an invading force of 30,000 streamed into the British territory of New Caledonia west of the Rocky Mountains.

War had not broken out again between the two North American rivals; rather, gold—"saint-seducing gold," as a poet said—had been discovered on the banks of the Fraser and Thompson Rivers, some 80 miles north of the line. The American fifty-eighters often made a disruptive debut in rude, quick-sprouting camps as they formed vigilante groups, destroyed property, and harassed local Indians. To a journalist from London their behavior confirmed the uncivilized character of Yankees: "They invaded . . . cornfields, ate the green peas, stole the oats, tore down the fences for firewood. . . . How strange that the natural coarseness, the bad manners, and the vulgarity of this people will cling to them wherever they go."

What was worse, the gold stampeders brought with them the possibility that the United States would annex the territory. More than twice as many Americans as British were camped on British soil. In London the Colonial Office did not sit still. Warships and marines were dispatched, and the Territory of New Caledonia was hastily upgraded to a crown colony with the new, proprietary name of British Columbia. Despite the agitation, thunderclouds never did break. Still, it was not until British Columbia joined the Dominion of Canada in 1871 that its citizens felt at all safeguarded from their southern neighbors.

During gold fever days it was not only stubborn north-south loyalties that fired passions; feuds also broke out between miners from opposite sides of the Rockies. The east-west division remains noticeable today, as the mountains mark for many a divide in outlook as well as geography.

"I've always found it easier to have mutual understandings with colleagues from Seattle and San Francisco than with (Continued on page 164)

Relic of a wave-whittled headland, a sea stack marks an earlier western shoreline of Vancouver Island. A wilderness of surf and sand and dense evergreen forest dominates both sides of the water boundary at the Pacific edge of the continent.

FOLLOWING PAGES: Mist mellows a sunrise vista of mountain ranges. From British Columbia's Highway 3 the view looks across the Selkirks, Purcells, and Rockies.

*L*ight airs, soft image: Poplar-fringed shore shimmers in Osoyoos Lake, one of three lakes that nourish British Columbia's famed fruit bowl in the dry Okanagan Valley. Settlers in the 1890s turned to irrigation to transform a bunchgrass rangeland into a garden spot with a million fruit trees.

Across a washboard of mountain ranges the border follows the 49th parallel to land's end, thence mazing through a sprinkle of islands and out to sea. In a boisterous dispute of the 1840s Britain claimed the line of the Columbia River (inset), while the U.S. reached north to the edge of Alaska with the threatening catchphrase "Fifty-four Forty or Fight!"

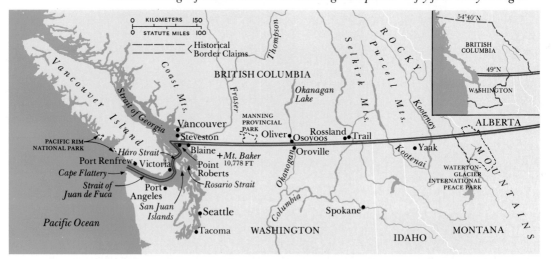

those from Toronto and even Winnipeg," remarked Arthur Erickson, Vancouver's celebrated architect. "In the east artists will build upon a body of knowledge and experience and carefully developed constructs. In the west they shoot off into virgin territory every time." Erickson believes the difference stems from the legacy of pioneer days. "Back then life demanded ingenuity at every turn. You couldn't depend on an established way; you had to do it yourself." For Erickson the "real rift" lies not at the mountains but at the Pacific Ocean: "The ocean softens the climate, changes the life-style."

Between the Rockies and the Pacific the 49th parallel traverses 300 miles of mountain ranges and valleys, one after another in accordion-like landscapes. A 19th-century pamphlet described the terrain as a "sea of mountains . . . all heaped together." Within the expanse the terrain ranges from semidesert where jack pine and sagebrush straggle up dusty slopes, to dripping rain forest where Brobdingnagian evergreens blot out the sun. Valley floors hold orchards and dairy farms, cattle ranches, and summer resorts. Above, on the slopes of the Rockies and nearby ranges, and in the Cascades and Canada's Coast Mountains, skiers and climbers witness a sublime canvas of alpine meadows and broad glaciers and a sweep of ancient volcanic cones, their peaks perpetually crowned in snow. Highest of the peaks within sight of the border, 10,778-foot Mount Baker seems to float above the clouds like Zeus's Olympus. In recent years the white cone in the Cascades has surprised scientists and area residents alike with intermittent spewings of steam and ash.

A decade or so before the gold strike of 1858 political spewings and rumblings broke out over how to draw a border west of the Continental Divide. The epic migration to the Oregon Territory had begun, and suddenly Britain and the United States were compelled to stake claims on the remote northwestern region. The British favored the Columbia River as a boundary, primarily for the access it afforded to the Pacific. To back the claim they pointed to the coastal explorations of James Cook and George Vancouver and to the early presence of fur traders for the Hudson's Bay Company.

As for the United States, a number of congressmen wondered whether the border should go past the Rockies. How could a fellow statesman from beyond the mountains even reach Washington, D.C., doubters asked. Popular sentiment, however, lay with the scheme to run the western border all the way up to the southern limit of Russian Alaska—latitude 54° 40′ N. Proponents based their position on the journeys of Lewis and Clark and the discovery in 1792 of the mouth of the Columbia by Robert Gray, who named the river after his ship.

Presidential candidate James Polk campaigned with the rabble-rousing slogan of "Fifty-four Forty or Fight" and won the 1844 election handily. Convincing Congress was another matter. Passage of the border plan required two months—one of the lengthier debates in the history of Congress. With their positions seemingly irreconcilable, both nations began making noises of war. Britain, however, felt more pressing concerns with her rivals in Europe. And affection for the disputed territory was not unanimous: Unlucky in his attempts to hook salmon, the British commander of H.M.S. *America* reportedly did "not think the country worth five straws." The United States, meanwhile, was anxious about impending war with Mexico. And so a compromise was struck in 1846: Extend the border on the 49th parallel from the Rockies to the Strait of Georgia, and then southward around Vancouver Island to the Pacific.

When I dropped down on the western side of the Continental Divide, I found myself one day at one of the mining sites that had drawn a flood of Americans. Here the deluge occurred in 1890, when gold was discovered on Red Mountain, six miles north of the border in the Monashee Mountains. Nearby, the town of Rossland—"the Golden City"—sprang up like a weed, with 42 saloons among its amenities.

"The border never meant that much here," said Jack McDonald, director of the Rossland mining museum. He was standing outside of the abandoned Le Roi Mine, which produced 30 million dollars in gold in its heyday—a billion dollars' worth at modern prices. Rossland was almost a suburb of Spokane, Washington, McDonald told me. There were so many Americans that the Fourth of July was celebrated, and there were identical funeral observances for President McKinley and for Queen Victoria.

Production hit a peak in 1902; thereafter the rich veins began "to pinch out" and a long decline set in. The miners left mountainsides pocked with shafts and an underground maze of 85 miles of tunnels. Skiers have now supplanted miners on Red Mountain, but on adjacent Mount Roberts a few solitaries work the tailings of old mines, convinced that the rocks still have riches to spare.

As in the past, miners deliver ore-bearing rocks to the town of Trail, a smelting center 2,000 feet below Rossland in the Columbia River Valley. Out of a dozen smelters in the area that once extracted gold from its encasings of copper pyrite and quartz, the one at Trail has survived to become one of the world's leading processors of lead and zinc.

Not far from Trail the Columbia River crosses the border. Having risen in the Canadian mountains 459 miles to the north, it flows through the United States for another 755 miles, emptying into the Pacific at the western extreme of the Washington-Oregon border. The river is one of the greatest sources of hydroelectric energy in the world. Fourteen dams—11 in the U.S., 3 in Canada—stitch its length. Grand Coulee Dam in central Washington backs up the Columbia some 150 miles to the Canadian border, forming Roosevelt Lake. The river's role as a power source as well as an aid to irrigation and flood control prompted the 1961 Columbia River Treaty between the U.S. and Canada. Under its provisions British Columbia built three storage dams on its portion of the river in return for sharing revenues from power generated downstream in the States.

Driving to the coast, I stuck primarily to the Canadian side. It was the only place where I found a road that strung along the border for any appreciable distance. What few roads exist in this knuckled terrain usually run north and south through the valleys, the same routes that the gold stampeders took to Canada. In the rugged Idaho panhandle, which adjoins the border for a scant 45 miles, I was warned to avoid the narrow mountain roads unless I had a citizens band radio in my car; otherwise an unannounced logging truck might leave me for scrap on a hairpin turn.

North of the Idaho line, it's caribou that sometimes pose a hazard. On an icy day near Stagleap Provincial Park, four caribou sauntered across the road, causing traffic to swerve to a halt. The animals belonged to the protected Selkirk Mountain herd, only 25 to 35 strong, and the last herd of mountain caribou to migrate into the conterminous United States. One of the four wore a radio collar, an aid to biologists on both sides of the border who study the herd's movements. Later that fall, a British Columbia hunter was fined $1,600 and stripped of hunting privileges for five years for shooting one of the caribou.

I reached the Okanagan Valley in late October. A broad trench that stretches for 150 miles through Washington and British Columbia, the Okanagan marks the dividing line between the Rocky Mountain system and the Cascade and Coast ranges. Entering the valley near the border town of Osoyoos, B.C., I saw roadsides and hillsides striated with the dense, orderly layouts of harvested fruit orchards—plot after plot of bare gray trees. From a distance it appeared as if a light fog hung in the valley. I also saw bird alarms mounted on tall poles; a single blast can empty an orchard of feeding birds. A month or two earlier the numerous roadside fruit stands would have displayed a cornucopia of local produce: apples, cherries, peaches, pears, plums, and watermelons. Now the stands still open offered but a few baskets of apples, pumpkins, and some shelves of cider.

The Okanagan Valley is one of the rare places along the border where winter is warmer on the Canadian side. Eighty-five miles long and as deep as 700 feet, glacier-dug Okanagan Lake acts like a thermal blanket north of the line. During the bright days of summer, the lake stores a great deal of heat. In winter the lake loses its heat more gradually than do the surrounding land masses. Come November the warm air rising from the water works as a shield against the cold air infiltrating from the Arctic. Temperatures in the B.C. towns of Osoyoos and Oliver often read five degrees higher than in Oroville, just across the border—where, incidentally, the spelling changes to Okanogan.

Harvesting by hand, workers snip plump clusters at the Inkameep Band vineyard on the Osoyoos Indian Reserve. The Inkameeps—a branch of the Osoyoos tribe—cultivate a dozen varieties derived from German and California grapes. Growers of the Okanagan and nearby valleys also produce apples, pears, and peaches—a third of Canada's fruit.

Canada's sunbelt, the Okanagan is the warmest section in the country, with 100-degree days regularly heating up the summers. Lying in the rain shadow of the Coast Mountains, the area receives only 8 to 12 inches of precipitation each year. With the introduction of irrigation the Okanagan has evolved from cattle country into one of Canada's richest fruit-growing regions. Since the 1950s the dry, sunny climate has attracted a sizable community of Portuguese, operators of the majority of orchards around Osoyoos. Add to the ethnic mix hundreds of French Canadians from Quebec who arrive each summer to pick the fruit. Directly south of the border migrant workers from Mexico harvest the plots.

While apples—chiefly McIntosh and Red Delicious—constitute the main cash crop, the fruit attracting the most attention is the grape. Situated in roughly the same latitudes as the famous vineyards in the Champagne of France and the Rhine Valley of West Germany, the Canadian half of the Okanagan marks the northernmost point on the continent where grapes are produced. It is also the country's largest grape-growing region after the Niagara Peninsula in Ontario.

Until the mid-1970s, Canadian vintages were widely viewed as "plonk"—inferior wine. Wineries crushed Labrusca grapes—a winter-hardy North American type—and came up with rough jug wines and cloying dessert wines that, according to one Canadian critic, created a "wine-for-winos" reputation. Labruscas, however, have been largely replaced by hybrids and by varieties of vinifera, the traditional wine grape responsible for the fine Old World wines. Nearly a dozen small estate wineries now offer their products in the valley, specializing in whites such as Gewürztraminer and Riesling. *(Continued on page 178)*

FOLLOWING PAGES: Wine on the vine, Okanagan Riesling grapes await the harvest and the vintner's art. They'll go to market as bottles of Inkameep White or Riesling.

*C*ascade high country: With every gliding step cross-country skiers kick up a spray of powder in Manning Provincial Park. Only 140 miles from populous Vancouver, the park's trails, waters, and campgrounds draw pleasure-seekers year-round. Across the border Mount Baker (opposite) soars to 10,778 feet—highest landmark within view of any point on this boundary. Distant Mount Shuksan, in North Cascades National Park, pokes through the sea of clouds.

*S*eascapes and mountain vistas surround the high-rise heart of Vancouver, one of the busiest Pacific ports in the New World. Climate and terrain allow Vancouverites to ski and sail on the same day, enjoy green lawns all year. Aerial view, below, looks north into the skyscraper thicket; farther north, 20 minutes away, an aerial tram (opposite) offers a superb look back from 4,000-foot Grouse Mountain.

PRECEDING PAGES: Rain adds luster to Gastown, once a civic blight, now a chic outdoor mall. Vancouver began here as a mill town. Picked for a railhead, it grew into a metropolis of 1.3 million.

*P*roduce market
overflows into the
street in Vancouver's
Chinatown. The lively
11-block enclave, largest
Chinatown in North
America after those of San
Francisco and New York,
tempts visitors with a
multitude of restaurants
and curio shops but houses
only 15 percent of the
city's Chinese population.
Chinese immigrants first
came to British Columbia
in the 19th century, many
as railroad workers.
Recent years have brought
East Indians, Japanese,
Italians, Greeks, and East
Europeans, who account,
in part, for the city's
growth.

Arthur Erickson, Vancouver's acclaimed architect, relaxes in one of his innovative masterworks. The airy Law Courts Building, part of a three-block complex that helped revitalize the city's center, rises seven stories to a glass roof. More traditional in his art, Jim Hart, a Haida Indian, carves a stylized salmon on cedar for a church panel.

Part of the credit for the turnabout goes to the Osoyoos Indians, largest grape growers in the Okanagan with 265 acres in cultivation. The vineyard garnered wide attention in 1977 as the site of the first large planting of vinifera grapes in the valley. A Canadian writer with an eye for irony reported: "If the experiment is successful . . . we shall see one of the niftiest role reversals. . . . The Indian will have brought good wine to the white man."

On a balmy fall day I drove through the trellised rows of grapes with Ted Brouwer, Dutch-born manager of the vineyard. "See," he exclaimed, waving his arm out the window, "we grow grapes where there are still rattlesnakes and scorpions." We stopped at an eight-acre test plot where 150 different grape varieties are grown to test their suitability to the Okanagan. Brouwer looked on as workers harvested the last grapes of the season, a Riesling variety imported from Hungary. So much sugar had accumulated in the plump green grapes that we, including Brouwer's cocker spaniel, ate them obsessively like candy. Seven years after the experimental planting, a third of the harvest is in viniferas. As to the future, Brouwer only shakes his head and repeats an Old World saying: "Luck and wisdom can't draw milk from a heifer. She's got to mature."

Before I departed the Okanagan, I stopped briefly at the brand new Brights Wines north of Oliver. Inside the plain brick building half a dozen Indians were racking white wine into four-liter plastic bags, containers that would soon be outselling bottles in Canada. In the lab I met wine maker Lynn Stark,

32, one of two women holding the title in Canada. Dark-haired, dressed in a white lab coat and blue jeans, Lynn walked with me into a cool, dark room lined with enormous stainless steel vats. Drawing off a few cloudy samples from red grapes recently crushed, she returned to the lab to check the contents for acidity, alcohol level, and other properties. "I wasn't a wine connoisseur," Lynn laughed, as we talked of her background. "I don't think I even drank wine in college. But I do have a really good nose for aroma and bouquet, which is very important." It took years of training to develop her tasting skills. Lynn smiled again: "Strange to think that you have to *learn* how to drink."

Somewhere near Princeton, B.C., I passed from the dry to the moist. It was as palpable and dramatic a border as I had crossed during my entire trip. Crossing the hump of the Okanagan Range, I came face-to-face with a Pacific storm front that typically was dumping its cloud contents on the western slopes, leaving high skies and dry air on the eastern side. Rain fell furiously, clouds were snagged in the tops of firs like torn bunting, and all of the sky was the color of wet cement. Welcome to autumn on "the other side of the mountains."

Not even the weather could dash my spirits when, after racing along the lush Fraser River delta with its strawberry bogs and mushroom farms, I entered Vancouver, Canada's hip and beautiful capital of the Pacific edge. More than four months and 1,800 miles had elapsed since Detroit, the next closest metropolis in the border vicinity, and now a mirage-like skyline beckoned.

I had heard that a few Vancouverites still bristle when reminded of the remark of a New York City mayor who described Vancouver as "that little village on the edge of the rain forest." But how could anyone take offense now? The truth is self-evident: Vancouver has blossomed into one of the great North American cities. Third largest urban center in Canada with a population of 1.3 million, Vancouver shines as a major transportation and distribution hub. Five rail lines, a web of highways, and a spacious harbor handle the outpouring of minerals and timber products from the British Columbia interior and the rich harvest of grain from the Prairie Provinces. A prosperous future was practically assured back in 1886 when Vancouver was selected as the western terminus of the Canadian Pacific. Today Vancouver ranks as Canada's only major city with direct access to the Pacific and the lucrative markets of the Far East.

With its glittery parapets of glass and steel and its air of conspicuous prosperity, Vancouver resembles other nouveau riche western cities—until the sun shines. Then Vancouver is transformed by its niche between sea and mountains into one of the world's most gorgeous urban settings, in the company of Rio de Janeiro, San Francisco, Hong Kong, and also Seattle, 120 miles to the south. Water frames the suitable-for-framing city on three sides—Burrard Inlet to the north, the North Arm of the Fraser River to the south, and the Strait of Georgia to the west. On a clear day frequent glimpses of deep blue water speckled with sailboats, ferries, and freighters bestow upon the city a fresh, aired-out quality, one that makes city living for once seem physically healthy. And befitting a metropolis in a nation that remains two-thirds wilderness, Grouse and Seymour Mountains rise right at the city's doorstep to the north, a magnificent backdrop 20 minutes away by car. Vancouverites justly like to crow that they live in a city where it is possible to sail, ski powder slopes, and play tennis all in a single day.

Vancouver is Canada's Riviera. With the exception of southern Vancouver Island, its climate is the most moderate in all of Canada. Mild temperatures come compliments of the Japan Current, or Kuroshio, a warm ocean flow that sweeps by the coast. Blessed by an incomparable location, city residents have developed a reputation for an insouciant, pleasure-oriented approach to life. Lotus Land and Narcissus-on-the-Pacific—these are apt nicknames for this corner of Canada. One morning I witnessed a telling scene: part of a race in which representatives of local restaurants, bottles of wine in hand, canoed, jogged, and bicycled 13 miles across town to see who would cross the finish line first with the year's earliest delivery of Beaujolais nouveau from France.

Like Toronto, Vancouver is unmarred by slums and, likewise, much of the tang of local life comes from a large, diverse ethnic community. On the city's East Side the cramped, neon-lit Chinatown was first occupied by some of the 15,000 Chinese imported in the 1880s to help build the railroad. The chic West End, with its forest of residential high rises, is notable for containing the most densely populated square mile in Canada. Residents practically step out of their front doors onto one of the ten public beaches within city limits. I saw a new thicket of buildings rising up along False Creek, an inlet that pinches into the city, as Vancouver was preparing for its 1986 World Exposition—Expo 86. In Gastown, the first permanent settlement in what is now Vancouver, boutiques and pricey restaurants inhabit spruced-up brick buildings, giving the area the look of a movie set for a turn-of-the-century costume drama. Even Indians, usually uninvolved in economic success stories, are sharing in Vancouver's high times. In the old, elegant residential neighborhood of Shaughnessy, a taxi driver pointed out to me a string of three golf courses on land leased from the Musqueam Indian Band. The metropolitan area includes four Indian reserves.

Musqueam villages and fishing camps dotted the shores of Burrard Inlet in 1792 when Capt. George Vancouver sailed his 20-gun sloop of war, *Discovery*, up a pocket of water and charted the site of the city that bears his name. Today grain elevators, oil tanks, and warehouses line the inlet. A radiant yellow mound of sulfur may brighten the end of a pier, contrasting with a white cone of rock salt or a hill of coal. Acres of logs pile up elsewhere on the waterfront.

Burrard Inlet turned out to be the city's greatest asset: an ice-free, deep-water port. Some 50 million tons of cargo come and go annually, making Vancouver one of the leading ports on the Pacific coast of the Americas. Coal and grain make up the primary exports, with Japan the principal destination; phosphate rock for fertilizer, salt, and sugar comprise the leading imports.

"Did you know some of Vancouver's charts are still in use? He was a perfectionist in navigation." David Drew tossed out this information as he and John Talbot, members of the port's harbor patrol, made the rounds of Burrard Inlet in a powerful motor launch. Drew and Talbot spend their shifts ensuring that ship discharges do not foul the harbor, spotting loose logs and debris that could become hazards to navigation, and generally keeping their eyes open along 96 miles of coastline. Drew illustrated one of his duties as the boat pulled up near the 643-foot *Valentina*, waiting to load potash for Japan. The ship, registered in Liberia, had requested permission to dump ballast. In a crisp, no-nonsense manner Drew reviewed harbor regulations with the freighter's captain. After visiting the deafening engine room to seal an oil discharge valve, he reemerged on deck to check the ballast. "If it has oil in it, it makes a discoloration on the water," he remarked as he leaned out over the rail to look. "It's clean," he announced and with that retraced his steps down the gangplank.

During the November fortnight I spent in Vancouver it rained every day. Normal for late fall. To live in Vancouver with its yearly average of 60 inches of rain—100 in the northern suburbs—one learns to accept the wetness, relieved that it is not snowing and all the more rapturous when the sun does shine, as natives assured me it does quite frequently in the summer.

Dwelling in a moist, cloudy climate does have the benefit, I suppose, of encouraging a refined sensitivity to shades of color and to the ever-changing gradations of light. For Arthur Erickson, Canada's best-known and most innovative architect, it is precisely the play of light that most influences his designs for Vancouver. A dapper, silver-haired man who retains offices in Toronto, Los Angeles, and Saudi Arabia, as well as in his native city where we sat and talked, Erickson explained how climate molds style:

"In Vancouver an architect has to work with very gray, soft light. This means that you must bring as much light as possible into a building, whether through skylights or walls of glass. You just don't punch holes in the wall. That creates a dark penumbra around a window that is very unpleasant in this town. You want a nice wash of light—a subtle transition from inside to out."

Erickson put theory into practice in dynamic fashion with his design for a three-block-long civic complex in downtown Vancouver. The focal point is the Law Courts Building, sheathed in an enormous glass roof that creates the illusion of sky as ceiling. The effect is at once so soothing and striking that the lobby of this modern courthouse is used to hold chamber concerts. The proud Erickson adds, "I've heard people say that it's almost worthwhile to commit a crime so you can go see the inside of the Law Courts."

Rain or shine, the city's most felicitous spot is Stanley Park, a thousand-acre forest and urban playground at the northern tip of downtown. In a sense Vancouverites should be grateful for the past belligerence of the United States. Fear of a backdoor attack by U.S. troops stationed in the Puget Sound area in the mid-1800s prompted British officials to set aside the site of Stanley Park for a military reservation. The remnant of virgin rain forest escaped the scythe of development and in 1888 it officially became a park.

In this lush and stately forest the real historical resonance of Vancouver resides. Towering Douglas firs and western red cedars are older than any of the surrounding buildings. And here the first inhabitants of the area lived and thrived for hundreds of years. One day in the park I encountered a young Indian stirring up the past as he went through the trial run of a tour which will include important Indian sites scattered throughout the city. Before the arrival of Europeans as many as 10,000 Coast Salish Indians occupied the shorelines and riverbanks of the Vancouver area, sustaining a rich and complex culture as they lived off the abundant seafood. Their descendants, the Musqueam among them, still inhabit both sides of the border in this region.

For most city residents the north rim of the park is known as the site of the Lumberman's Arch, a monument commemorating the British Columbia timber industry. For Victor Guerin, 20, a Musqueam with black, shoulder-length hair, the association is different. He knows that in this area stood an Indian winter village called Whoi-Whoi. "As recently as 1862, 700 people lived here, and there were perhaps a dozen longhouses," Victor announced to an audience of Canada geese and a TV crew. "The people lived off beach foods—clams, crabs, mussels, sea urchins—and went back into the forest to hunt land animals."

The villagers left a shell midden 20 feet high; the mound was leveled when the first park road was built, with shell remnants used for the road surface. As Victor went on practicing his tour narrative, anthropologist David Rozen, an adviser from the Museum of Anthropology at the University of British Columbia, pointed to the frosty ground. Looking closely, I could see fragments of shells strewn through the thick grass. Traces of Whoi-Whoi still exist. "Ninety-nine percent of Vancouver doesn't know about this archaeological site," David said as I picked up a fluted scallop shell. "Joggers don't even know that they're running past it every day."

So the spell of Lotus Land kept beguiling me with its revelations and pleasures; finally, however, I had to break away to finish my ocean-to-ocean border journey. The end of the line—that is, the 1,287th and final mile of the land border on the 49th parallel—comes at a pinch of land known as Point Roberts, Washington. A geographical fluke, Point Roberts dangles below the 49th parallel at the southern tip of a peninsula, cut off from the rest of the U.S. mainland. Children ride buses 32 miles through British Columbia to reach school in Blaine, Washington. In the 19th century Canada openly desired these five square miles of woods and beach for reasons of logistical common sense. But the United States refused to negotiate.

Today, British Columbians are just as happy that Point Roberts stayed American. The reason became evident one Sunday afternoon when I walked into a Point Roberts bar and found hundreds of Canadians gulping beer and cheering Canadian football on TV. With bars closed in British Columbia on Sunday, Point Roberts, 30 miles south of Vancouver, becomes overwhelmed one day a week with Canadians seeking a public drink. By my lights Point Roberts was the Tijuana of the north, an enclave of attractions not easily available on the other side. Canadians come across not only to partake of Sunday refreshments, but also to watch X-rated movies (banned in B.C.), play bar bingo (banned in B.C.), and buy gas (38 cents cheaper, I noted). A million cars cross the border yearly into a community of fewer than 500 people. And with Point Roberts receiving half as much rainfall as damp Vancouver, Canadians have bought up more than half the land for vacation homes.   *(Continued on page 188)*

International Peace Arch, built on the boundary near its western end with money raised by schoolchildren, enshrines the hope that open doors between the nations will never close.

FOLLOWING PAGES: Home for the winter, the Steveston fishing fleet—more than 700 craft, nearly half manned by people of Japanese descent—throngs the town harbor south of Vancouver. A U.S.-Canadian commission regulates salmon fishing in the area.

*V*ictoria *looks the part of a city named for Great Britain's queen. Fine imports, such as the china, Dresden figurines, and Sèvres vases opposite, fill numerous shops in British Columbia's capital. In the benign climate a golfer sinks a putt in December—the winter green as green as springtime. Tracery of lights and Washington's Olympic Mountains in the distance lend enchantment to the Parliament complex, completed in 1897—a jubilee year for the queen, her 60th on the throne.*

To the south of Point Roberts lie the San Juan Islands, where British and American troops dug in during a famous boundary dispute of the 19th century that came to be known as the Pig War. In support of the British claim to most of the archipelago, the Hudson's Bay Company established a sheep farm on San Juan Island. American squatters eventually settled on the island as well. In 1859 an American farmer dispatched a Hudson's Bay pig that had trespassed on his potato patch. From this trivial incident the dispute festered until both nations landed troops on the island. The U.S. garrison was led for a time by George Pickett, who would later head the fateful Confederate charge at Gettysburg. But there was no suicidal charge on San Juan. For a dozen years the two military forces held their ground, the standoff leavened occasionally by socializing between troops from opposite sides. In 1872 the emperor of Germany, acting as arbitrator, awarded the islands to the United States.

Just as the international border enters the continent by water in the east, riding up the middle of Passamaquoddy Bay, so it departs by water in the west, following the Strait of Juan de Fuca out to sea. The western boundary leaves land at a point midway between the wave-drenched cliffs of Cape Flattery on the Olympic Peninsula in Washington, and the forest-mantled coast of Vancouver Island in British Columbia. At night lighthouses from opposing shores 12 miles apart blink at each other, as if in recognition.

It was in the timeless rain forest of Vancouver Island that I ended my six-month journey along the border. To reach the wilderness I rode a ferry across the Strait of Georgia to Victoria, capital of British Columbia and bastion of nostalgia for most things British. The city resembles an attractive theme park with its half-timbered houses, a dozen teahouses, "shoppes" selling English china and tinned sweets, the Union Jack flying from the venerable Empress Hotel, and waiters who pronounce "tomato" as Professor Higgins would. Victoria donned its disguise in the first half of this century when British civil servants favored its temperate climes for a retirement haven. Today the Merrie Olde England facade is maintained mostly for tourists; the retiree community now comes mainly from Canada, especially the Prairie Provinces, the newcomers bringing with them long memories of bone-chilling winters.

The charm and amenities of Victoria seemed a world away instead of just the width of Vancouver Island when I reached the isolated fishing village of Port Renfrew. Four other hikers and I had gathered to embark on the West Coast Trail, a spectacular, grueling 44-mile path through thick forest and along rocky shores. "An irresistible hell," according to one description.

"You're crazy!" a bystander shouted above a downpour as we lowered ourselves into a wide-bottomed herring skiff that would take us to the trail. We probably were crazy. Storm front after storm front had been sweeping into the area. As we set off for the two-mile trip across the inlet of Port San Juan, torrents of rain lashed down on us and whitecaps exploded over the sides of the bucking boat. We pulled our rain gear tight and held on.

Capacious M. V. Coho *awaits cars and passengers at Port Angeles, Washington, for the 90-minute ferry ride across the Strait of Juan de Fuca to Victoria. From here many travelers head to snowy peaks, rain forests, and beaches of Olympic National Park.*

FERRY
TO
VICTORIA

M.V. COHO
ONE ROUND DAILY DEC 1st THRU DEPARTURE 8:30 AM
TRIP MARCH
SHORTEST ROUTE TO CANADA

We landed on what looked like a boneyard. Dozens of tree trunks lay heaped on the beach, bristling with splinters, the bark chewed off as the trees gnashed against each other. "The winter storms really pulverized these shores," outfitter Bryan McDicken reported after a reconnaissance. He stood by a cedar tree, 150 feet of it, that had been uprooted and flung here by the sea, the snaggle of roots spread out like wild, matted strands of hair.

Because of the heaving sea the beach was impassable even at low tide, and we retreated into the gloomy forest to find a campsite. From all around came the sound of water—the deep-throated whoosh of breakers, the sizzle of fast streams, the ceaseless dripping from boughs. Before we fell asleep the sky cleared enough for us to make out the snow-streaked mountains of the Olympic Peninsula and a low band of light from the village of Neah Bay, both across the Strait of Juan de Fuca in the United States.

For six days we slogged along the trail. The weather was so wet that photographer Mike Yamashita resorted to an underwater camera. The few times when we could walk the beach we picked our way across stranded logs and around severed pieces of kelp; occasionally seals craned their necks out of the tumultuous surf to watch. We leaped over some surge channels, forded others, and at times used slippery logs as bridges to cross rain-swollen creeks. Bryan told us that on sunny summer days hikers observe gray whales, pluck a meal of crabs out of tidal pools, and splash beneath a waterfall. How could we believe him?

The sight of logs being tossed like matchsticks recalled the tragic history of ship-bashing along this stretch of coast. Ships and fishing boats rounding Cape Flattery into the Strait of Juan de Fuca have been seized by treacherous currents and driven against the rocky shelves of Vancouver Island. Since the 1850s some 60 vessels have foundered here. In 1906 the loss of 126 people in the wreck of the *Valencia* roused the government to order a decent trail hacked out along the coast for future shipwreck survivors.

We spent most of our time on the old lifesaving trail, driven there by the sea and rain. Moss hung in tatters from giant hemlocks and 800-year-old western red cedars. Fungus the size and texture of a child's baseball mitt jutted out from glistening trunks. Lime-green light filtered through the treetops. The lifesaving trail came under the jurisdiction of Pacific Rim National Park in 1970, and since then park authorities have reduced the number of hazards. Thus we climbed into cable cars and pulled ourselves by rope pulleys over ravines, and walked across other gorges on swaying suspension bridges. Boardwalks had been laid across bogs, though many of the boards had rotted, sending us up to our shins in muck. Not even our expensive, brightly colored rain gear could keep us totally dry. I wondered if the Indians who once lived here had had any better luck with their waterproof clothes fashioned out of cedar bark.

About midway to Bamfield, the village at trail's end, we came upon a hallucinatory sight: a freshly painted cottage sitting in the midst of a manicured lawn behind a white picket fence. The vision turned out to be the grounds and living quarters at the Carmanah Point Lighthouse. Farther on, near the deserted Indian villages of Clo-oose and Whyac, we spotted a curl of smoke and traced it to a lovely shingled cottage beneath the trees. Located on one of the last remaining private inholdings along the trail, the house belonged to Jim Hamilton, a writer,

Northern sea lions loll on a rocky island in the Strait of Georgia. Their feeding habits at times disrupt commercial fishing—depleting the catch and damaging gear. Canadian fishermen may shoot them around nets. Some 5,000 California sea lions—a different species—migrate each year to winter in British Columbia coastal waters.

and his 79-year-old mother, Dorothy Ordway, who have lived on the property on and off since 1952. After half a lifetime in the rain forest Jim still felt humbled and awed by his surroundings. "We have just two city lots here, a postage stamp in the wilderness," Jim said. "And in the winter, with no one else here, there's the illusion of living on another planet."

For the rest of the day I kept recalling those words. Backpacking through an overgrown forest, with thoughts of danger and physical challenge monopolizing the mind, it was hard for me to remember this planet's U.S.-Canadian border—the quiet little towns embracing across the line, the spacious lakes and intimate white-water streams split into two countries, the ever-present customs stations, the trim swath cut through forests and over mountains.

The border is a creation of history and politics, of sovereignty and diplomacy, but here in a rugged, extravagant wilderness, such concepts and conceits seemed no more comprehensible than the distance to the stars that shone faintly through the torn clouds. That night the wind gusted madly and the surf boomed like thunder. From my tent I drowsily looked out at the dark outlines of four figures bent over a leaping fire. Soon I was imagining that I was lying in a rain forest 10,000 years ago.

"Of course, there's a border," I began mumbling, "of course, there's a border . . . of course. . . ." And then I was asleep.

*T*ime out for surf watching: A backpacker pauses on the driftwood wrack during a six-day hike beside a "graveyard of the Pacific." Used as an escape route for shipwreck victims, Vancouver Island's West Coast Trail winds 44 miles through forest and swamp and along steep slopes. Hikers ladder down the face of Valencia Bluff (opposite upper); just offshore 126 died when a reef ripped the Valencia in 1906. On a soggy day—routine for this rain-soaked coast—low tide makes the going easier (opposite).

FOLLOWING PAGES: Cape Flattery Light on Washington's tiny Tatoosh Island has guided vessels into the Strait of Juan de Fuca since 1857. Frequent rain, fog, and gale winds make the passage a mariner's nightmare. The 3,987-mile border, which splits the strait, ends between Tatoosh and Bonilla Point on Vancouver Island.

Acknowledgments

The Special Publications Division gratefully acknowledges the invaluable guidance of our project consultants. Dr. Alec C. McEwen, Canadian commissioner on the International Boundary Commission since 1976 and a student of border history, served as chief consultant. Others included Dr. Richard Beach, Director of the Center for the Study of Canada, State University of New York, Plattsburgh; Dr. Howard Jones, associate professor of history, University of Alabama; and Dr. William E. Lass, professor of history, Mankato State University. We received encouragement and assistance also from Frank E. Whetstone, United States commissioner on the IBC, and from the commission staff. Other agencies that were frequently consulted include the U.S. Geological Survey, the U.S. Customs Service, Energy, Mines and Resources Canada, Parks Canada, Revenue Canada/Customs and Excise, Statistics Canada, and the St. Lawrence Seaway Development Corporation. The editors also wish to acknowledge the assistance of many other individuals mentioned in the book or cited here: Duane W. Barrus, Robert Berg, William J. Berg, Robert N. Bergantino, Bob Berrisford, Frank Bevacqua, Stephanie Bolchalk, Peggy Brody, Jean A. Brookins, Linnea Calder, Debbie Dick, David Elder, Frank Fenderson, P.M. Gerwing, Gary E. Glass, Brian A. Hodge, Mike P. Hofer, R.D. James, Helen Kerfoot, Simon Lunn, Frank McArthur, J.G. McCrea, Teresa Mitchell, Clyde R. Moore, B.P. Neary, Keith B. Neilson, Lynn Osmond, Donald and Kim Prangley, Elvira Quarin, Frank Saprowich, Charles B. Sigler, Paul Smith, Nydia Vargas, Tim Watson, Patricia Wilkie, and Lester G. Zeihen.

Additional Reading

NATIONAL GEOGRAPHIC magazine has published many articles dealing with the peoples, places, and natural history of the U.S.–Canadian borderland. Consult the cumulative index. Valuable information about the border and its political history was also gleaned from issues of *Canadian Geographic*. In addition, the following books proved useful in the preparation of this volume: Pierre Berton, *Why We Act Like Canadians;* Jean Bruce, *The Last Best West;* H. George Classen, *Thrust and Counterthrust;* John Robert Colombo, *Colombo's Canadian References;* Don E. Fehrenbacher, *The Era of Expansion: 1800-1848;* Robert T. Handy, *A History of the Churches in the United States and Canada;* Bruce Hutchison, *The Struggle for the Border;* Howard Jones, *To The Webster-Ashburton Treaty;* William E. Lass, *Minnesota's Boundary with Canada;* Richard B. Morris, *The Peacemakers;* W.L. Morton, *Manitoba: A History;* Guy Murchie, *Saint Croix: The Sentinel River;* The National Film Board of Canada, *Between Friends/Entre Amis;* Grace Lee Nute, *The Voyageur's Highway;* John E. Parsons, *West on the 49th Parallel;* Donald F. Putnam and Robert G. Putnam, *Canada: A Regional Analysis;* Frank Rasky, *The Taming of the Canadian West;* Elwyn B. Robinson, *History of North Dakota;* Erling N. Rolfsrud, *The Story of North Dakota;* William Toye, *The St. Lawrence;* Jessie and Wreford Watson, *The Canadians: How They Live and Work;* and George Woodcock, *Canada and the Canadians.*

Soaring barrier of the Rockies marked the end of the boundary during the second quarter of the 19th century. After settlers surmounted the barrier, so did the line, pushed west, by agreement, along the 49th parallel.

FREEMAN PATTERSON/MASTERFILE

Library of Congress CIP Data
O'Neill, Thomas, 1951-
  Lakes, peaks, and prairies.
  Bibliography: p.
  Includes index.
  1. United States—Boundaries—Canada. 2. Canada—Boundaries—United States. 3. United States—Description and travel—1981- . 4. Canada—Description and travel—1981- . I. Title.
E179.5.062 1984   973   84-22775
ISBN 0-87044-478-6
ISBN 0-87044-483-2 (lib. ed.)

Composition for *Lakes, Peaks, and Prairies: Discovering the United States-Canadian Border* by National Geographic's Photographic Services, Carl M. Shrader, Director, Lawrence F. Ludwig, Assistant Director. Printed and bound by Holladay-Tyler Printing Corp., Rockville, Md. Film preparation by Catharine Cooke Studio, Inc., New York, N.Y. Color separations by the Lanman Progressive Company, Washington, D.C., and Lincoln Graphics, Inc., Cherry Hill, N.J.

Index

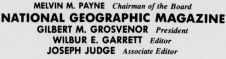